Reflections and Memories of an Amish Misfit

Reflections and Memories of an Amish Misfit

My therapist says that's not true, but I digress.

Mary Byler

COPYRIGHT & DISCLAIMER

Disclaimer: This is a work of memory and flashbacks based on Mary's life. There are many events and details that have not been included due to the severity and nature of the trauma. Some names, characters, places, and incidents have been modified to prevent vigilante justice (per advisement). Except for the already convicted abusers any resemblance to actual persons, living or dead, events, or locales should be presumed to be coincidental.

This is also not written to say all Amish are bad, its written because Amish are just people and some of them commit crimes.

Copyright © 2022 by Mary Byler

All rights reserved. No part of this book may be reproduced or used in any manner without written permission of the copyright owner except for the use of quotations in a book review. For more information, please send your request to the following email address: anamishmisfit@gmail.com.

First paperback edition December 2022

Cover design by Mary Byler & Jasper Hoffman

ISBN: 978-0-578-27675-5 (paperback)

www.themisfitamish.com

DEDICATION

THIS IS DEDICATED TO ALL WHO HAVE TRAVELED A LONG, LONELY AND OFTEN DIFFICULT ROAD. YOU ARE NOT ALONE!

TO THOSE WORKING IN MEDIA OF ALL TYPES AND IN ACADEMIA WHO PROMOTE THE ACCEPTED NARRATIVE AND ERASE THE EXPERIENCES OF THE MOST MARGINALIZED WITHIN AMISH COMMUNITIES, I HOPE YOU LEARN THE TRUTH FROM MY STORY.

Table of Contents

Title	i
Copyright	v
Dedication	vii
Acknowledgements	xi
Reviews	xiii
The Plain People	xv
Foreword	xvii
Introduction	xix
Content Warning	xxiii
Chapter One	1
Chapter Two	14
Chapter Three	34
Chapter Four	48
Chapter Five	63
How can you Help?	103
Epilogue	105
Writing and Art	107
About the Author	123

Acknowledgements

To my partner and family, I could never have written this without your kindness, support, and love in my life.

To my chosen family, I love you and I am so grateful to be here with you, I couldn't have done this without your support and help.

To Misty Griffin who pre-read and gave feedback. Thank you so much for your honesty and compassion. Your friendship means the world to me.

To the folks at Into Account, A Better Way, and The Plain People's Podcast for their support during this time.

To the survivors that pre-read this and provided insight and feedback. Thank you for bearing that burden and helping me put this out there. I appreciate you.

To the people who showed up for me throughout my life, sometimes the smallest act has been the thing that I've been able to hold onto that kept me alive and going.

To the driver that helped me escape, you changed my life for the good in a different and better way than what I ever dreamt possible.

To the people that believed in me, when I didn't believe in myself, you helped me more than I can ever express.

To all the survivors throughout the years that have encouraged and provided support,

To the people who showed me what actual support and love is,

To the people that check in on me when I fade,

To the multiple people that helped me edit, Aspen Rayne, Tara Mitchell, and Rue Layne,

To the Copy Editor: Andre Swartley,

Thank you

REVIEWS

"I just finished your book and feel it is very well written. It really took me back to another time in my life and as hard as it was to read about the horror you endured it is very inspiring to see the way you literally are coming back with buckets of water for those still in the fire. I feel the cultural aspect is accurate as there are many of the smaller details, I can very well relate to having seen and experienced them growing up. And the schools and those problems are still very real. Long story but our girls are now in safe school."

-Anonymous Amish Person

"Mary's story cements the Queer Amish experience in a community that silences LGBTQ voices."

-James Schwartz, Author of "The Literary Party: Growing Up Gay and Amish in America"

"The culture was spot on, I felt like I was transported back to where I was Amish again.

It's a story every single person on the planet 16 & older should read."

-Misty Griffin Author of Tears of the Silenced

THE PLAIN PEOPLE

Being Plain is not synonymous with being Amish. Being Plain defines a group that practices a Plain life, which may include plain dress, even if they're not specifically Anabaptist. There are many varieties of Amish and even more Anabaptists, but not all are Plain groups.

Some Anabaptists go to college and some you wouldn't be able to define as Amish or Anabaptist by their dress or their mode of transportation.

Not all Anabaptists are Plain. Not all Plain people are Anabaptist.

Check out [The Plain People's Podcast](#) for Plain Peoples stories.

[Misty Griffin's](#) book: [Tears of the Silenced](#) is available on Amazon

[A Better Way](#) is an organization that focuses on Education & Training for Child Abuse Prevention and Survivor Support.

[The Misfit Amish](#) have research, blog posts and podcasts that tell the stories of Anabaptist and Amish people. We bridge the cultural gap.

FOREWORD

If you believe that all Amish people are incredibly good and should never face criticism for anything, my story is not for you. You should find another story to read that puts them on a pedestal. Don't bother reading this book!

Throughout the years, since I have started speaking publicly against abuse in Amish Communities, many people have written and published articles about me that are inaccurate and have discrepancies that tell only the story they want to tell. This is me, telling you, what I want to tell you about being born Amish.

Because my first language was PA Dutch, some of my story is told in PA Dutch. Where necessary, an English translation is provided the first time a PA Dutch word is used.

INTRODUCTION

Dear Reader,

Imagine living with these memories popping up as various flashbacks as you go about your day and in your night terrors as you sleep.

Never ending, despite utilizing various methods of trauma therapy for PTSD for over 19 years.

All it takes is a scent, a touch, certain words and/or actions, emotions and you're transported to relive one of the most traumatic events of your life, repeatedly.

I was born the sixth child and the only girl. My parents had three more sons born after me. When my dat (dad) passed away, my mem (mom) remarried a widower seven years later and I gained nine stepbrothers and five stepsisters that were all significantly older. One stepbrother with a disability lived with us until he passed away. My stepfather and my mem had one child, my sister.

I come from people with large families, anywhere from four to sixteen children, which means I have hundreds of first cousins and lots of aunts and uncles as well as distant relatives.

I lived in five different Amish communities in Wisconsin and Pennsylvania. This book is organized by community.

Because Pennsylvania Dutch is my first language, there will be scattered Pennsylvania Dutch throughout this book. I provided translations behind the first time I used the phrase. Just be aware that some things do not translate appropriately from

Pennsylvania Dutch to English and therefore the phrase or word may lose or change meaning. Native Pennsylvania Dutch Speakers also may use English different than native English speakers. Please keep that in mind as you read.

This is my accounting of Amish experiences in the communities I lived in that I am willing to disclose at this time. Names have been changed and any similarities to specific people are unintentional. I became convicted that it is time for me to write about the experiences that I had in various Amish communities after, yet another person wrote about my experiences inaccurately.

This conviction could also be a normal effect after recording two seasons of Plain Rainbows which tells the stories of LGBTQ Amish and Anabaptists. Each of our guests stories has deeply impacted me and helped me reach a place where I feel compelled to speak my truth, my way.

This is a chronological sequencing of my memories of growing up Amish to the best of my abilities.

Trauma often causes memory issues for people; events may lack details, others may seem out of sequence, but it is important to understand that this is how childhood trauma can affect anyone. These events may not make sense to you, welcome to flashbacks and night terrors I live with.

I had multiple abusers throughout my Amish life, but I want to say this to all of you. Please examine the elements of abuse I discuss; most of my abusers were older children.

Consider this:

What type of environment does a child grow up in to think abuse like this is normal?

What type of behaviors were modeled that children think it is normal to sexually assault one another?

A note about rehabilitation: Research has indicated that children who commit sexual crimes but receive rehabilitation from qualified and licensed facilities and mental health providers for sex offender rehabilitation before reaching adulthood have the most likelihood of never re-offending.

I love my Amish family, I always have, I always will. Loving my family doesn't mean I have to destroy myself mentally to be present in their lives on a regular basis.

Abuse was reported to hopefully facilitate interventions that would allow them to receive appropriate interventions instead of interventions from people that did not have the knowledge and skills necessary to provide sex offender rehabilitation.

I invite you dear reader to sit with your discomfort and find out where you stand on the issue of combatting child abuse in America?

Ask yourself carefully,

Am I part of the problem?

Or

Am I part of the solution?

Choose wisely, the answer can't be both.

Thank you!

Mary

CONTENT WARNING

This book describes various experiences I had as a conforming Amish person from birth until 19 years of age. This is a story of childhood trauma and survival as a born Amish, queer, neurodivergent and assigned female at birth (AFAB) person.

Please be aware there is abuse of all sorts contained in these pages.

If you find yourself in distress, please stop reading until you are ready to begin again.
If you're in distress, you may also reach out to:

National Sexual Assault Hotline: 1-800-656-4673 OR
https://www.rainn.org/

Suicide and Crisis Hotline:
Call: 988,
Text: 988, OR
Chat support is available on their website: https://988lifeline.org/chat/

The Trevor Project:
Call: 1 (866) 488-7386,
Text 'START' to 678-678, OR
Chat support is available on their website: https://www.thetrevorproject.org/get-help/

Chapter One

ABE TROYER AMISH

March 20-21, 1984-1989

"You own everything that happened to you. Tell your stories. If people wanted you to write warmly about them, they should've behaved better."

— *Anne Lamott*

Imagine with me: not knowing the exact day of your birth, being told it was around midnight, but everyone present at your birth forgot to annotate the time of birth. I consider this the stage on which I entered the world, not important enough for my first breath of air to be noted.

The home we eight children, and our parents, lived in was divided into three sections: a barn, a leather shop, and small living quarters. Out front was the leather shop, the barn was on the side. We did not have enough bedrooms, so I slept on a cot in my parents' bedroom.

Everyone around me was talking and I opened my mouth, but it didn't form words. Eventually I had a medical procedure called a Frenotomy to correct the Ankyloglossia (a congenital anomaly passed down from one or more parents), I was born with. After that procedure I could talk, especially with my mem (mom) as much as I wanted to.

Mem laughed and said, "Maybe they cut it too much...," since I was talking to her so much.

I would hide under the table with our border collie Laddie while laying on him in the hope that he wouldn't leave while I was sleeping. This memory comes up frequently and makes me wonder what else might have happened to me that I don't remember but made me so fearful that even my dog would abandon me.

At one point us children were taken outside, and we lined up in a row to take turns shooting a twenty-two gun with our dat (dad) supervising.

Going on Sunday afternoon walks was good during summer months on our in-between Sundays. (Amish church is often every other Sunday, the non-church Sunday is frequently referred to as in-between Sunday.) We'd all walk down to the creek in the woods, and I saw a crab there. I was a little scared of it, but I wasn't alone. I was with my mem, dat and my brothers. We were simply fine.

We'd watch the tadpoles in the creek sometimes. It was good to watch and see how quickly they turned into frogs. Our father caught a snapping turtle in the creek and our mem dutifully cleaned it and cooked it up. Sometimes, we'd catch frogs in the creek, and she'd cook up frog legs too.

We had a corner outside our house where the toads would come jump around and play. My brother and I would go catch the toads and hold them. Later, when I had warts all over my hands and fingers, my mem said it was because of me touching toads.

I remember the joy of biting into the fresh bread I'd helped my mem prepare by pounding my little fists into the dough. That first bite of warm bread was glorious, and I loved it.

I watched my oldest brother stand on a stool at the wasserbank (water bench, means kitchen furniture made by Amish when they're not supposed to have kitchen counters with sinks in them). Suddenly, he fell off the stool he was standing on to wash dishes and he shook on the floor for a while.

I asked mem, Vas is letz mit da Mosie?
(Mom, what's wrong with Moses?)
Mem: Ehr grickt spells.
(Mom: he gets seizures)
I asked mem: Was mainst?
(Me: what do you mean?)
Mem: Wan ehr an babie var, var ehr grank, so grank mit so hoch en feva es hot ein weh geh du in si kop, nah grickt er imma spells von sel. Mi hen ein zu da ducter gnoma van di nachbara gsagt hen si zilla di law calla van vi ein net ni nemma. Sin an da hospital ganga. Er hat spinal meningitis ghat.
Mom: When he was a baby, he was sick, he had such a high fever, it harmed him in the head. We took him to the doctor when the neighbors said they would call the law (cps/DHS?) He was in the hospital with spinal meningitis.
Me: Ok.

This is also the place my brothers had a skateboard and got reckless with it. One of them knocked his head in an accident and was bleeding. I remember being terrified.

Example: Amish Coloring book

I was so happy coloring any pictures I could in my coloring book, the crayons made me want to explore them. I loved the way they smelled, so I stuck one in one nostril and another in my other nostril. I tried so hard to get them back out, but I couldn't. I couldn't breathe so I ran, terrified to my mem for help. My mem tried desperately to get them out, but she couldn't either, so she took me to my dat. My dat pulled a pair of needle nose pliers from one of the leather working benches and extracted them. I felt so relieved I could finally breathe again, and that my dat had made it better.

I had chicken pox when we lived in the house with the leather shop in front, and I itched myself all over in discomfort constantly. Later, I had the mumps. My face was swollen and painful. I felt so yucky, and I didn't want to move or play. (Some Amish people don't believe in vaccinations, therefore us children had a few more childhood illnesses than our "English" neighbors).

I loved to go play in the leather shop until one day an English woman walked through the doors of the leather shop. She spoke kindly to me and even though I didn't understand what she said, and I followed her everywhere. She was beautiful, and I decided I was going to grow up and marry her, or at least a woman like her. My dat then took me into the living quarters where I told dat and mem that I was going to marry a woman, then got hit with the belt.

Shortly after, I was startled awake as dat climbed into my bed. I can't describe here what he did to me, but he hurt me very badly. Later, I told Mem "He did bad things to me."

His response to Mem's questions was "I took care of it." Mem told me to never talk about it-"He's sorry and you must forgive him."

"But Mem, what does forgive mean?" I asked.

My Mem replied, "To forgive means he's sorry and you can never talk about it. If you do, your sin may be as big, if not bigger, than his sin."

My mem also rebuked me for how I withdrew from my dat and didn't speak to him. I didn't go into the leather shop anymore. I didn't sit on his lap. My mem encouraged me to forgive him and endorsed me sitting on his lap even after I told her of his abuse. I didn't have the words then to describe that I was terrified of my dat and even when I talked about it no one would hear me.

I rocked side to side in the corner. Wishing for a box to rock in. I knew if Mem saw me, she would make me stop, so I hid. But just maybe if I had a box, she would allow me to rock inside the box until it fell apart.

Sometimes, I crawled into bed with my mem. She made me feel safe and didn't hurt me, and soon I drifted off to sleep. I startled awake, still lying next to my mem- my dat touching me in inappropriate places and doing inappropriate things. The next day when I told my mem, she said she would talk to dat.

I didn't dare fall asleep next to my mem anymore.

One Saturday afternoon my mem told me to undo my braids. I hated the braiding that happened once I got them out and after Mem helped me wash my hair. Like all girls under twelve in all five of the communities I have lived in, my mem would braid my hair once a week. My braids were tied off with yarn, done tight enough to last a full week twisted up underneath my Kapp. This Saturday I went to my mem's treadle sewing machine, an antique Singer with a foot pedal and cabinet attached and found her Gingher sewing scissors- and cut off both of my waist length braids. The relief was worth both the scolding and the following belting. (In all five communities I lived in young girls under the age of twelve would have their hair braided once a week either by their mem or an older sister or other women able to braid their hair. It was left in for a week at a time and the braids were tied off with yarn and put up underneath a Kapp).

I remade the doll like the one I remember playing with.

My mem sewed me a bop (doll) without a face. My brother and I played church with my bop. He'd get up and preach. I'd sit on the bench and take care of the baby. I wanted to preach too, but my brother and mem said I can't, it's just not done because women and girls don't preach, "Men were created first and women were created second," so di frau muss still si. The women must be silent. I named my bop, Ella. My mem told me "We don't name our dolls, they're not people." I cried. My bop was my friend, I talked to my bop daily.

We would go to church every other Sunday and some Sundays we would go to our dawdies (grandparents) for a meal. There would be a lot of uncles, aunts, and cousins there. My cousin Leah would play with me sometimes. The older cousins would get us to pick blueberries from my aunt and uncles blueberry patch that they had fenced in. They'd lift us young ones up and set us down inside the patch and we'd share our blueberries with them. My momi (grandmother) had a candy room and she would have us grandkids line up and we would get to choose a piece of candy from her stash. It remains one of my fondest memories.

Our neighbors at the end of the lane had a dog named Max, Max was a Doberman pinscher and my brother had sleepwalking nightmares about this dog. (Now I wonder, what did my siblings experience in this home). The neighbor across from them was a little old lady, that I just loved, but she was English, and I couldn't communicate with her.

Her grandson broke into her house one day and he had guns on him. We went to our other neighbor's house who were in contact with law enforcement, and we had to follow their directions to stay safe from this guy with guns breaking in someone's house. While we were there, our neighbor turned on the tv, I remember my mem saying something and me feeling like the devil was in TV. I was terrified of TV now too.

Occasionally, the neighbors across from us would have my mem and several of us children over. They had a child my age that I was able to play with. This child and I couldn't talk to each other, but we found ways to connect through playing with her beautiful dolls. I loved them so much. They had faces, — mouth, eyes, ears, and hair. I was content driving them around in her toy car, while she played next to me with another doll.

One Sunday on our way home from somewhere there was a porcupine in the road. The horse shied away and my dat got out of the buggy. The porcupine shot quills everywhere eventually.

One of my older cousins was married and had a baby. I got to go with my mem to see the baby. Her baby was adorable. I loved my cousin and her baby so much.

The haymow was a lovely place to go smell the hay and play. It was hot up there, but good. I didn't hear my mem calling me from there. My brother came running and told me "Mem zillt da dat saya, van du net grad na kommst" (Mom will tell dad if you don't come right away). I saw dat's belt hanging up on the wall and I didn't want to feel the belt again on me so I ran to Mem as fast as I could.

It rained around me and I went into the house so I would not get wet. Our mem and dat called for us children to come outside, to see the rainbow. They told us how this was a symbol of God's promise, since he destroyed the world in a flood and God would never do that again. It's a symbol of hope that he sent his son to die for our sins and now we might be able to live our lives in such a way, we can only hope to get to heaven.

Abe Troyer Amish
Description of the accident that killed my dat, my uncle and my cousin in The Pittsburgh Press, May 4, 1989

The Pittsburgh Press

LOCAL NEWS BRIEFS

Amish man, boy die as truck hits buggy

An Amish man and his nephew were killed and another man injured when the horse-drawn buggy in which they were riding was involved in a collision with a pickup truck last night in Warren County.

Killed were the driver of the buggy, Abe Byler, 37, of RD 3, Sugar Grove, and his nephew, Daniel Byler, 7.

Daniel's father and Abe's brother, Eli, 31, was in serious condition in the Women's Christian Association Hospital in Jamestown, N.Y.

Although details of the accident weren't available, state police said the accident occurred at 8:15 p.m. along Route 957 in the northern part of the county, about two miles south of the New York border.

Police said initial indications are that the buggy was struck from behind by a pickup truck driven by Ricky Jones, 33, of Logan Road, Warren, who was not injured.

Daniel was pronounced dead on arrival at the hospital and his uncle died a short time later.

Job Fair May 18

Job Fair '89, which will bring together job seekers and career advis-

---

On May 3, 1989, my dat, uncle and my 7-year-old first cousin went fishing. They did not come home when we thought they would. We saw flashing lights over the hill. Our mem gathered us, and we all got on our knees and prayed together. Eventually, law enforcement came and told us there was an accident. A truck had hit their buggy, it was smashed, the only intact piece was a wheel, the horse was thrown 150 feet and dead-on impact. My cousin was killed on impact. My dat died that night and my uncle died the next morning. A neighbor took us to the hospital, and we sat there. I was with my mem at the hospital.

The strangely dressed and talking people (Law Enforcement Officers) came and talked to my mem about the accident. I heard Amish adults talking about how the driver was zoffa (drunk), and the world wanted us to prosecute, but we don't do that as Amish. I don't know if the driver was successfully prosecuted, nor do I know if he was driving under the influence, but that is what I was told.

There was a large funeral to bury all three of them together on May 7th, 1989. I didn't quite understand why everyone was so sad. The bad guy in my night terrors was gone. I didn't cry over him dying until sometime in my teens and even then, it was because of the grief that, he should have been a safe person for me to be around. I was a small child, and he wasn't safe for me.

The buggy only had oil lanterns for lights. Soon after the accident this community switched to battery operated lights on their buggies.

The community did not like that we talked to our English neighbors that I mentioned earlier. After the accident, they had a big auction and sold our leather shop, our home and property. We moved across the community to a house near my dawdies on my dad's side. I never saw my English friend again.

My cousin was a little bit older than me and that summer we decided to go hide in the woods between Aunt's house and grandpa's house. We hid while we watched everyone searching for us. Eventually, we did come out and we were spanked soundly, and we were not allowed to play together for a long time.

My aunt was a single lady (they called her an old maid) and she had a loom shop. She would go in and weave rugs and sometimes I was allowed to watch and or help her. It is one of my fondest memories.

On our Sunday gatherings at dawdies house, I remember my momi, a 4-foot eleven-inch woman getting in my uncle, the bishops face about something. I don't remember what, but he cried, and she said her piece. It really stuck out that women can speak! My momi was not for the faint of heart. My mem often told me throughout my life, "You are just like her."

Glass beads I strung in memory of momi

When we went to dawdi's house during the week, sometimes I got to watch momi string beads. She had a tray and a string as she quickly strung those beads so fast. It was magical to watch my momi make these beads. They were beautiful, and she would give them as gifts when people had babies. It is customary for many Amish to not have baby showers, but when the baby is born, people visit the family with the new baby, and they may bring beads like this or a dress for the baby. (In all 5 Amish communities I lived in baby boys also wore dresses).

There were disagreements that I overheard and saw. The disagreements were partially because my mem did not agree with Momi practicing braucha (magic) between my mem and my momi, which I never understood. Then again, I was five years old. I am sure I will never understand their relationship. Shortly after that we moved to another community that was an Old Order Amish Community.

Today, I am proud to carry my momi's spirit. I am proud of our ability to speak. I get to speak in a way that makes sense to me, and I feel my momi inspired me so much to keep fighting against oppression by her determination to use her voice. We get to speak our truth and that is meaningful to people.

When I remember these events or they get brought up by events transpiring in life, I often think about the grief I have for the child I was. The isolation and inability to communicate with people. I was born tongue tied and they had to do surgery to correct it when I didn't talk. I don't know how all these facets affected the way that I experience life and the impact of these events, but I can tell you I wept.

I screamed.

I prayed.

I had faith.

I believed.

I practiced conformity.

I was modest.

I tried. I tried so hard.

Chapter Two

Old Order Amish One

1989-1994

"People always say that I didn't give up my seat because I was tired, but that isn't true. I was not tired physically... No, the only tired I was, was tired of giving in."

– *Rosa Parks*

We moved into our dawdies' house in this new community. My aunt, uncles and cousins lived in the adjoining house. The dawdi haus was small. (It is common for many Amish to have a small house attached to a larger house and the parents live in it, we call it a dawdy haus) There was a cellar to do laundry in, a kitchen, a living room, and upstairs there were bedrooms and a door that went through to my aunt and uncles upstairs where my cousins would be.

In this community, men only wore a certain type of blue chambray and white shirts made by their mothers or wives, with a laydown collar, but not like the English style lay down collar, men had no suspenders on their pants. Women and girls wore complicated dresses with tucks along the bottom, and the capes were worn somewhat like an x with a square in the center of the x in the front, sewn a specific way and then folded and pinned with straight pins the church approved way. Women and girls were allowed to wear more colors, but not too light and not green, however purple was allowed if the material was only one type, and it was opaque. I learned to hold up the material on my arm with the sunlight shining through to determine if the material was opaque enough to be used. I also learned not to wear shiny fabric.

When the adults including my aunt, uncle and mem went visiting other families in the community, my older cousins would be responsible for me. My older cousins would lock me in their bedroom and then my 18+ year old cousin would climb in through the window and rape me. I begged my cousins not to do this to me, but they still did. The three of them laughed at me as I screamed, the terror my little heart knew was awful. I was wetting my bed every night. My cousins mocked me for this and because of the dawdi house being small, I had to sleep in the room with my older cousins. I don't have words for how awful this was.

In the fall, I'd bundle up and ride on the wagon pulled by a team of draft horses out to the field to husk corn by hand with my cousins, I was tired and grumpy because it seemed like we were out there all-day husking corn by hand.

Sometimes. I'd bundle up and go out to the barn at chore-time and play with the kittens. Two of my cousins then found a way to get me in the haymow and rape me on multiple occasions. I screamed uncontrollably when my mem instructed me to go to the barn.

Dawdi often hit us grandchildren with a large stick, and we all knew to hide from him when Dawdi would go trim the lilac bushes because we knew someone was about to get a whooping. He had no qualms in disciplining his grandchildren. I spent considerable time finding hiding spaces from dawdi. One of my best spots to hide was to climb in the snowball bushes and hide there. I couldn't hide there anymore when the leaves fell off it, since dawdi could see me in the middle of the bush.

One Sunday afternoon we went for a long walk to the woods and saw all the leaves changing color. There were birds singing and flying around. Out past the back forty we went in the tunnel under the highway. It was fun to go in tunnel and yell loudly, I loved listening to the echo. Near the tunnel was a natural spring and we waded into the creek and drank from the spring by the falls. It was the best!

One of my female cousins took me to the basement and I cried because I didn't want her to touch me. (Note: trauma survivors may have specific memories that don't include everything that happens but retain the feeling of crying or emotion that goes with it. I don't have words for how this made me feel, even today).

There was a big brick wood oven outside. The week before church at my aunt and uncles house, women baked loaves of bread, apple pies and moon boi (half-moon pies). We also cooked apple butter in a large kessel with a wood fire under it in the wintertime. I loved the bread, apple pies, moon pies and apple butter. These were my favorite things.

We had to be careful not to dirty up the house as the women and girls cleaned and cleaned for weeks prior to church. Every window was washed to be sparkling clean, all the curtains were taken down and washed, starched, ironed and re-hung, the kitchen cupboards were cleaned inside and out, the furniture was all washed along with the walls and ceilings. The basement was cleaned out, all the woodwork was cleaned, the floors were scrubbed and, in some places, we would be scrubbing the woodwork with a brush to get up all the dirt. The doors were cleaned and the silver was polished, the pots and pans were scrubbed. It was a big job to get ready for church.

The Sunday church was at my aunt's house, I sat on the backless wood bench beside my mem. It wasn't so bad as the singing began, the ministry got up and went upstairs to a room. When the ministry returned, then the preaching began, we prayed on our knees, next the Deacon read from the Bible in High German. (I couldn't understand it). The minister kept droning on in his preaching. I was so tired of the noise. More preaching and a second prayer. Then the bishop announced where church would be in two weeks, lord willing, and we had more singing before it finally was over. (An Amish church service is usually around three to four hours long and four times a year we had two church services that were around six to seven hours long)

During church I often swung my legs and clasped my hands together as I tried not to fidget, but I failed and my freshly starched apron became wrinkled quickly as I started thinking about the forest, the birds in the forest, the creek with the spring in it and the waterfall as the minister's droning faded out. The creek with the falls was a beautiful place and I was there when I was jarred back to church by everyone kneeling in for prayer. My mem often had to tell me to kneel. I was so happy when the last word was sung, and the boys and men filed out of the house. Finally, I could move again without getting in trouble. It was time to prepare for lunch though, so the men came back in and set up two benches together and a bench on either side as the women would set the tables. I will never forget the men smoking their pipes in the living room after church, so much that the room was blue with smoke. I was fascinated watching the smoke in all its patterns.

The women spread out a bowl filled with cut up bread, then cooked seasoned navy beans with brown butter put on top and hot milk, also seasoned was poured over it called gma soup. They added apple butter, butter, bread, pickles, pickled beets, and apple pies with a moon pie. A bowl of soup was centered between four people and all four women and girls would eat directly from the bowl. After the silent prayer before we could eat and the men started eating, there was coffee and tea sent around. I was happy when I finally got to eat because I loved gma soup and I still do. After we were done eating, everyone bowed their heads in another silent prayer. If not everyone had eaten yet, the women and girls would clean dishes and refill the food so that the next group could eat. The women and girls would clean up all the dishes and take care of the food and the men would break down and pile the benches once the tables were cleared. After the dishes were all washed, dried and put away I could try to play with other girls my age. Sadly, I don't remember being welcomed. Instead, I was mocked and not played with for having warts on my finger and hand. It was confusing to be so alone and surrounded by people.

We had a garden this year; I remember the delicious tomatoes and green onions. I would go into the gardens with my older cousins but eventually that too became unsafe, and I laid in bed and cried and cried.

I struggled with suicidal thoughts daily as young as 6 years old. It was a constant never-ending battle, and I prayed to die.

Soon we moved into a new house near the dawdi house where I didn't have a bedroom. The attic was unfinished and one large room. I slept in the attic with my brothers in this room. Sometimes my mem would let me sleep with her, but mostly she made me sleep up there where the horror was, and I absolutely hated it. I sleepwalked. I cried so loud during my sleepwalking episodes I would wake myself up. I would wake up in this house underneath the stove outside on the closed porch, confused and having no idea how I got there. I wasn't safe where I was sleeping. The night terrors, sleepwalking and trouble sleeping were frequent. There was nowhere to escape it. I was forced by my mem to sleep in a room with my rapists.

One day, we came downstairs, and our mem was in bed with a tiny little baby boy, he was so sweet, innocent, and adorable. I loved him so much because I could play with him; he was too young to think I couldn't do anything right because I was a girl. I played with him for what seemed like hours at a time. He was adorable and so cute. I wasn't supposed to hold him too much because "Holding babies too much spoils them," Mem said.

My first school

Amish people have a religious exemption (Wi V Yoder, 1972) so they can stop sending their children to school after eighth grade instead of High School.

This resulted in Amish one room schools that don't teach science, evolution, sexual education etc. The church and the schoolboard heavily moderate curriculum content. Books may have pages removed, passages marked out with a marker, pages stapled together or even glued together. Many, but not all, of my schoolbooks were published by our church approved publishers.

I started school in 1990, when I was 6 years old. It was a basic one room school, with about thirty-six children and usually one, sometimes two teachers. Grades 1-8 were taught at this school. We would play games on the field at recess time. Tag was good for all of us. In the wintertime we played in the snow outside at recess. If we were lucky, we had a cheese sandwich wrapped in foil to put on the wood stove to eat for lunch. It was nice to have something warm when it was so cold outside.

When my mem, my brothers and I went to someone's house for dinner, my school bullies were there. When I went to the outhouse, I saw awful things there. I screamed I was so terrified. I got in trouble for screaming. Everyone I saw doing terrible things denied it.

I had an accident (wet myself) in front of the entire school at the blackboard when I was writing on the blackboard. I was afraid of going to the outhouse since I saw girls go in there and then the boys went in and I would sometimes hear screaming and more. None of the adults did anything about this. I wasn't safe at home or at school. I didn't have any friends at this school. Children mocked me and hurt me all the time.

Old Order Amish One 1989-1994

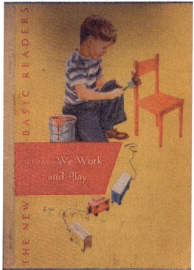

One of the books I read at this school

The snow blew outside as I watched through the windowpane, I couldn't go to school, I was either cold and shivering or hot and feeling awful. I itched at the red bumps on my skin. My mem said we had measles, and they were a childhood illness, and I must stay home from school. I wanted to go to school so I could learn to read more as we were reading the Dick, Sally, Jane books and I loved finding out what was happening next. It let me forget all the awful and imagine a world where I wasn't hurt so many times. It lasted for over a week, and I hated it, I was so glad when I felt better and went back to school and found out what happened next in the books. This was the third preventable childhood illness I had.

I was fighting with my brother again. My mem pulled up two chairs and made us face each other and sit on the chairs until we apologized and were ready to play nicely. I never wanted to fight with my brother again.

One of my brothers fell out of the swing in the tree and had a big hole in his head that gushed blood. He had to see a real doctor to get stitches in his head and alas I couldn't swing there anymore as the swing was taken down.

I happily skipped side to side. Skipping was fun. It made me feel at one with myself despite everything. I often did it while sucking on my thumb.

For as long as I could remember I sucked my thumb to fall asleep or whenever I was experiencing dreadful things. If I was happy, I sucked my thumb, if I was sad or mad, I sucked my thumb, it was something that helped me regulate my emotions to be acceptable in the environment I was in.

Sucking my thumb was not considered acceptable for me as I was considered old enough to conform to societal expectations. Regardless, I didn't stop sucking my thumb, I just stopped sucking my thumb around people when my mem put cayenne pepper on my thumb. This was the last one I remember but previously, she had put other things on my thumb that just didn't matter to me. I sucked my thumb despite all of it. I did it every night to go to sleep and whenever I was alone.

I was so scared; My mem and I were getting on the greyhound bus with so many English people to go somewhere. It was cold. I shivered in my mandli (cape for little girls) even with my coat underneath and my kopduch (headscarf) under my kapp (covering). I awoke with a jolt as we got off the bus and waited for another one inside the station. I was so curious, my mem told me to not look at the screens and not to let anyone take pictures of me as we don't believe in graven images because of what the Bible says. This part is fuzzy, and I don't think this is the mode of transportation we used every time I went to this Amish doctor. We eventually arrived in Indiana at an Amish doctor's place. We had to wait for a long time for our turn to go in. My mem told the Dr about me wetting my bed and some other things. He prescribed tincture drops, vitamins, and herbs. My mem said it wasn't normal for children my age to wet their beds every night like I still did. My mem also said the nightmares were bad and maybe we could do something. After that she gave me herbal capsules that were supposed to help me sleep without nightmares. Remember most Amish people are only allowed an eighth-grade education.

Old Order Amish One 1989-1994

Example of the nail clipper

When we got home, I sat on the bench beside the table with my hand out. I watched as my mem put vitamins and herbs in my hand, then held a nail clipper on a chain over it. If the nail clipper went around one way, I wouldn't have to take the vitamin or herb, if it went the other direction, I'd have to take the herb or vitamin. She went through about twenty different pills meanwhile I sat wondering how this worked.

What would make the nail clipper know if I had a deficiency in my body and needed these vitamins or herbs?

When I got older, I used the nail clipper for myself to do this to be obedient and take the vitamins and herbs that mem said I needed to take it wasn't long before I saw that the way the nail clipper swung yes or no, depended on my thoughts. I tried to talk to my mem about it, but it didn't matter.

I was really scared when I started passing out. I passed out three times, that I remember when I was a child. I do not recall seeing a licensed medical doctor in this community about this issue. Today I now know that PubMed research indicates some of the herbs I was given may cause dizziness.

Despite multiple visits and multiple different tinctures, herbs and vitamins recommended by the Amish doctor, I still woke up screaming from the night terrors and having wet my bed.

When I was around 7 or 8 years old, one day my stomach hurt so bad, I cried all the way as I walked two miles to school one way. When I came home that day, my mem asked me questions. My mem took me to a licensed medical doctor the next day. The nurse took me to another room away from my mem, I didn't understand what she was asking me, so she brought mem in to translate for me. When she asked if anyone had touched my private areas, I said yes. My mem lied to them. She answered no when I said yes. She told me you don't talk about that to anyone. I was so confused. I didn't understand how we are not supposed to lie, but when it comes to English people, now we lie and its ok.

At Christmas time, we did a gift exchange at school and had a school program where most of our families showed up. I sang happily "We wish you a Merry Christmas" with all the other children. The older children got up and recited poems. After we sang the last song, we got to open our gifts.

As I learned to read and write English, I learned to draw pretty letters eventually. I loved drawing things instead of working on my schoolwork. I loved coloring books; it was so good to watch the picture come alive with color and meaning.

The way certain markers sound when you write with them hurt my ears in school. Children would sometimes put their nails on the chalkboard which hurt my ears too. When I was in school it was so loud and overwhelming, I cried often because of it.

We moved to a house in a different church district. For the first time in my life, I had my own bedroom. This was shocking and a welcome change. It was a tiny little room, but it was my room. This was a long brick house, with a big living room, a bedroom downstairs, a kitchen, an outhouse, the upstairs had three rooms on one side and one spacious room on the other side. It was obviously an English home at one point converted to an Amish home.

I don't remember specifics about this, I just have fragments of going in a van to three different Amish communities where we had distant relatives and spent time at their houses. One of them was in a different state. It was a separate way of doing things too. Even though I was scared to go, it was better than being at home.

Another fragment of memory is going to an outdoor farm where wild animals would come up to the vehicle we were riding in, the people driving it had included food for the animals. I wanted to be a wild animal and run away.

Soon I went to the dark outhouse in this place and my brother was hiding in the darkness and proceeded to rape me.

"Mary," my brother called, "come"! I dutifully got up and ran towards my brother. He was in the spacious room upstairs. He had two of my other brothers with him. I thought to myself, I would be ok since he wasn't alone. I went closer as he asked me to. He directed my other brothers to hurt me in specific ways as he watched. I screamed, I begged, I prayed, I wore my kapp forward, I tried to obey always, I believed, I was submissive, I tried to always keep my dress down as my mem instructed and the preachers preached. Nothing worked. I was still at the mercy of this brother.

My second school:

When I started a new school, I had one friend there sometimes. Meaning sometimes she played with me. And there was Rachel. Rachel also played with me sometimes and we walked to and from school together if we could. One afternoon, Rachel and I decided to go to the dump instead of going home. Oh boy, we got in trouble for that. Another time we hid in the cornfield instead of going home. We got spanked for that and grounded from playing together because we were bad influences on each other. When we walked home with the boys, sometimes the boys would throw rocks in the air and hit people. I don't know if it was an accident or on purpose.

My other friend at this school, Rebecca, was the daughter of someone who became ordained in the ministry, and once her dad became ministry, we weren't allowed to play together as much.

Sometimes, I would click my four-color pen over and over, but someone would put a stop to that quickly. Then I started picking at my skin. I still pick at my skin today.

The teacher here was the best teacher I had in all my Amish years of schooling. She found unusual ways for me to do things that made more sense to me. I learned ways I could learn at this school and loved reading. I read the whole school library. This teacher helped me find other ways to do things and understand that sometimes having to do things differently than others doesn't make me wrong. Since I felt I was wrong for everything I did, it was helpful to have such a kind teacher. People around us openly called her an old maid.

This teacher also got in trouble with the church for telling us something about dinosaurs. There were games the children played at recess, sometimes resulting in children being sexually abused in front of each other. She banned those games and tried to make it stop.

When spring rolled around, we would walk to school barefoot. My shoes had holes, so it was nice to not wear shoes with holes in them.

Clop, clop, the sound of the horse was monotonous and lulled me to sleep in the buggy. We were on the way to visit my poor aunt. She had gotten up one morning and her husband and three of their children were gone. Si sin fatsprunga (they had run away) from the Amish. I heard adults say my poor aunt was mentally ill already. Schizophrenia they said it was. She just made things up, now with this, she might have another episode requiring hospitalization. So, people went to visit her for a while. She was so sad and cried, but to me she was amazing. I loved her. She was so kind to me; she spoke to me like I mattered.

On the last day of school, our families came, and we played games, had races, and roasted hot dogs on the bonfire that our parents built outside. Having hot dogs was a real treat and made me so happy!

By this time, I was aware that the church had assigned men to manage the stipend they gave my mem for us children.

Our garden didn't do so well that summer. We didn't have a large crop from the garden and one fall day Mem was at the neighbors (one of the men in charge of her stipend) asking for assistance, when one of my brothers played with matches and our furniture in the living room caught fire.

Two of my brothers and myself were in the big spacious room upstairs. We were playing and talking and one of my older brothers called me from downstairs. I was terrified to go. So even though my brothers went downstairs and made it out, I couldn't go because I knew it wasn't safe for me to go when I was called. Because if I did there would be somebody lying in wait.

So, I didn't go right away. And then, when I saw the smoke coming up the stairs, I just decided that I would just die from the smoke. It'll be easier that way. So I went into my tiny room that was the size of a twin bed. I was sitting there, resigned to die. But it took too long. Soon I heard the sirens from the fire engines, and I realized they were just going to put the fire out anyway. I was still going to be alive, and I would have to see some strange men, and that terrified me more than anything. Then I remembered my brother that played nicely and kindly with me. I decided to try to get out of the burning house.

There was a window there that had nails attached to the side so that it couldn't be opened. I eventually got the window open and jumped out of the second-floor window and into the cornfield. It was scary, but what followed made me long for death and pray for death.

My brother went to a hospital in another state due to burns from the fire and the community sent us children to different homes. Our mem went to the hospital in the other state. I was sent with my one brother to Aunt Hannah's house. My aunt had children of her own and was married to a minister in the church. I was to work to earn my keep. I was 9 years old. Tasks I was to complete included carrying in wood, helping make food, pack school lunches, sweep and mop the floors, clean the windows and more.

I hummed as I happily cleaned the bedrooms upstairs until there were new assailants in the bedrooms. As I was going to carry wood, I would experience even more horror. I fought, but I was never strong enough to protect myself. I couldn't go to the outhouse here. This memory stands out vividly: walking past the wood piled up all neatly to go to the outhouse and getting to the outhouse to someone lying in wait to rape me.

As I packed the school lunches, I hummed, I had to use cheap bologna to make myself and my brother sandwiches as instructed to do by my aunt. I also wasn't allowed to give us all the same food as my cousin's lunches. I made separate lunches for my cousins with healthier food and more food than what I was allowed to pack for myself. I tried to sneak my cousins food into my lunchbox one day and my cousin ran home and told her mem. I got hit for that.

My brother was soon sent elsewhere, and I was alone in the house of horrors (with the people who proclaimed themselves my saviors).

When we ate together, my aunt didn't allow me to eat the same food as everyone else at the table. She said, 'it cost too much to feed me."

When I was mopping the huge living room, my cousin sat there reading a book and watched me clean.

When I was sleeping, a female sexually abused me here.

My aunt Hannah was upset when I went back with my mem after the church built us a new house. She said, "But Mary, wasn't it so nice here?" I wanted to throw up. Nice for you Aunt Hannah?

The new home was the nicest home I had ever lived in. It was fresh and a brand-new chance to live. It wasn't long before it, too, was tainted by people waiting in the darkness to hurt me. I locked myself in my bedroom, but it didn't stop anything from happening to me. There was no safety. I told my mem.

After I told mem, the threats became worse, there was grooming that went on, random little nothing gifts to this day make my skin crawl.

The threats:

I will kill myself (to an adult this is horrifying, to a child it is a godawful way to manipulate them).

I will kill you.

I will run away from the Amish and then there's no hope my soul will go to heaven.

Many nights, I cried myself to sleep praying to die. Since my dat died, my mem didn't want me, and my brothers were raping me. If there is a God, why would he/she not hear the anguished prayers and let me die?

I was lucky though because now I had a small chihuahua puppy. Her name was Penny. She really helped me sleep in my own bed, when my ears hurt so bad, I crept as silent as possible, down the stairs and tried to go get my mem, except the door was locked to go downstairs, so I went back to bed and sobbed to Penny about my ears hurting so bad.

Before this my mem blew smoke in my ears when I had an earache and put garlic in my ears, then she added a cotton ball. Nothing really helped and I never saw a doctor about it. (My ears still bother me, and I am unable to see a doctor about them). I couldn't understand why she stopped caring about me.

Sometimes I would sleepwalk downstairs and climb in bed near Mem, sometimes she would let me sleep in the bed with her and other times she would let me sleep on the floor down there. I didn't feel like my mem really cared about me anymore. I was afraid to sleep, and I started sneaking books I wasn't supposed to read to my room, where I would read them quietly until late in the night.

People butchered all winter long and brought us the livers to eat. We didn't have enough food that winter. Our mem went in the cupboards, got lard, milk and flour, and made us rivel soup.

There were times my stomach hurt so much from not having enough food, I'd cry myself to sleep at night. One night I climbed out of bed and crept down the stairs to get my mem and the door was locked. I cried and cried since I was locked upstairs, and I didn't understand why my mem didn't care.

Oil Lamp on the nightstand in my room

I whistled as I was getting the chimneys on our oil lamps in the bedrooms upstairs, turned around to leave and go downstairs and there was my brother, blocking me from leaving. We had an altercation that made noise. I heard my mem call "Mary, vas is letz?" (Mary, what is wrong?) as he put a finger over his mouth and shh'd me and whispered "You better do as you are told and pretend like nothing is wrong. You just broke the chimney by accident. Or else." Terrified, I did what I had to, he then proceeded to further harm me in ways I can't describe here. I don't have words for this. I cried as I was hit with a rubber hose for breaking a chimney because I wasn't careful enough. I knew if I didn't comply with his demands, I would surely die and suddenly, I wasn't sure I wanted to die at his hands.

There was an English man who came around after the new house was built and he had bought me a Barbie doll, I wasn't allowed to have it. Later, my mem said, "You're too old to be playing with your bop," and threw her in the living room stove and burned her. She said, "It's time for you to work."

We were soon preparing to move to another community where my aunt and uncle were planning to move to. As we prepped for moving my mem decided that we couldn't take Penny with us, and she gave Penny to an aunt of mine.

Today, I am thinking of the ways I coped back then. Let me tell you some coping skills were unhealthy; however, I had and still have no words to describe what emotions I felt.

Anger was preached against; it was a sin that could send you to hell, to burn eternally. When I laughed, my mem said, "Musz net so laud lacha" (don't laugh too loud), and that "all ihre lacha vat sich verkehre in weine" (all your laughing will end in crying.) Sometimes I screamed when I was being hurt but I would get beaten for it. I learned it was futile to attempt to express any emotion in any way when it came out and I was hit to break my will.

One thing I learned was to whistle; I was so proud I learned how to whistle! I whistled all the time. It was great and gave me a better feeling inside.

The preachers in every Amish community I lived in would preach that you must break the will of the child in the highchair. That meant if a baby was sitting in the highchair and didn't put their hands under the table, the parents (and if the parents weren't there, the caregivers) were obligated to hit the baby's hand against the wood to break their will. Or if the baby was restless and squirmy on the mother's lap during church for example, the mother was responsible to leave the room with the baby and hit the baby to break their will. For to love your children is to not spare the rod, lest ye spoil the child.

One of my brothers wanted to chew tobacco, my mem got him chewing tobacco and when he took a big old chew and put it in his mouth it made him sick, and he threw up. I was disgusted as I cleaned up the vomit.

My brother and I decided one day to try smoking our first cigarette down behind the barn, except we didn't have any cigarettes, so we made a corncob pipe and put tea leaves in it. Ah, yes, we told each other as we coughed. That was so good.

My brother and I knew we didn't want chewing tobacco, so yes, we also sang a forbidden song, "Smoked my first cigarette, down behind the barn." Later I learned Little Jimmy Dickens recorded this song. I still sing along with pride when that song comes on. I may not be a great singer, but I love singing and singing has been a way to express things for years now. Forbidden songs helped me understand feelings eventually and express my feelings.

Since I knew some English songs, I sang them as I went about doing my chores. I'd scrub the washboards singing "Farther along, we'll know more about it, farther along, we'll understand why, cheer up dear brother, live in the sunshine, we'll understand it all by and by" which I learned later was written by William B Stevens. I had no idea who wrote this song as I sang it. I wondered what the songwriter had experienced in life. The message of understanding why in the future gave me hope that someday I could understand why.

Today, I understand there are things that I will never fully comprehend and that's ok. Later, one of my therapists asked me this:

"Do you know that to understand why people commit crimes can mean you're capable of committing and justifying the same crimes?"

What could make any human being deserve these kinds of crimes?

What could a child do to deserve these crimes? The answer is nothing. Children are not sexual beings; they don't sexualize things. It is adults who teach each other and sometimes children to sexualize other children. Children are often curious and want to explore the world, but they can also never consent to sex or intercourse since they do not have the brain development to fully grasp the consequences of sex or intercourse. We can and must do better than this.

While I've always desired to know why, I'm ok with not knowing, now that I've processed this in therapy.

This song, though, helped me hold onto hope for a better future as a child. It still comes to mind, and I still sing it. Having hope is critical to my mental well-being. Training myself to hold on to hope was important.

I've learned that having moments of despair can creep up on you. Sometimes it feels like it steals my joy like a thief in the night and I'm back there in this environment, where no one cares about children's safety.

Throughout the years therapists and trauma survivors taught me different tools to try to help me refocus on the present moment and not live in the trauma that encompassed so many aspects of my formative years. (For the record, people typically ask me for permission prior to offering any potential tools as an option).

One of the most effective tools I've found is to remind myself of the changes in the way society talks about Amish child sexual abuse cases. We have a long way to go to create meaningful change that will ensure an environment of safety for every child in the world.

But we have come a long way from where we were the moment, I escaped my community.

I remind myself that if we can come this far, humans can do anything, we try different approaches and ways until we smash the barriers into smithereens.

I remind myself it's a marathon, not a sprint.

I remind myself no child deserves what I and others have survived. We are not invisible. We are visible. We are not silent. We Speak, we get together and when we do that, we raise awareness in a meaningful way for those who may not be in a place to speak, we don't speak over or for them, we speak for ourselves.

This is our power. We take back our power.

Together, we rise from the ashes of the torture they put us through.

Together, we are the change.

Together, we lift our voices and speak truth to power.

I am NEVER alone in this journey again.

YOU ARE NOT ALONE!

WE   ARE   NOT   ALONE!

Chapter Three

Old Order Amish Two

1994-1996

"I learned that courage was not the absence of fear, but the triumph over it. The brave man is not he who does not feel afraid, but he who conquers that fear."

— *Nelson Mandela*

When we moved to this community, I had no idea that it would be the most liberal Old Order Amish Community I would live in. We moved in the dead of winter, and it was cold. I'd walk to school even when it was cold and blustery. If we were lucky the English school bus driver would come along and give us a ride to our school nestled in the valley.

This house had several bedrooms upstairs, and one downstairs but still not enough bedrooms for everyone. There was a pantry in a corner of the kitchen we called a fauli maud (lazy maid), I loved to run the pulley and lever that would put the food in the basement and bring it back up when needed. It was so neat and such a helpful thing to have. I had never seen one before.

In this community men wore light colored shirts of a variety of colors and suspenders; they also had a different haircut than the previous communities. Women and girls wore different dresses than either of the previous communities. Their capes were like the Abe Troyer capes in several ways. The kappa (multiple coverings) were different than either of the communities prior to this. I was so happy when my mem sewed me a new cape that was longer and warmer.

This house was near another family and got outdated food that we were able to eat. It was better than the Rivel soup and liver that was all we had to eat for a long time. My stomach wasn't hurting when I went to bed most nights. I would put my carton of milk outside in the snow at night before I went to bed, it would freeze overnight, and I got to have icy milk in the morning as it thawed.

We made ice cream here. It was delicious! I really loved making ice cream with our hand cranked ice cream maker with ice and salt. We went sledding on the hill behind the house when it snowed and there was no school. The sledding was so fun!

At school, I didn't talk to anyone because I talked to one girl when I first got there, and she turned me in to the teacher for using too many pieces of toilet paper. This makes me think about the stomach trouble I have had my entire life. Let's not even talk about being a kid and bleeding when I pooped. But I used six sheets of toilet paper because it was bleeding and there was still poop. When I was reported, I got in big trouble with the teacher and my mem gave me a talking to about not using too many pieces of toilet paper.

Schoolchildren were hit with a big paddle by the teacher at the school, and we would hear it smacking and the child being hit would cry. I didn't want to get that discipline for using too many pieces of toilet paper.

The Amish owners of our house had a son who was getting married, and they were planning either that he would live in the house with his new wife, or they would move into it themselves. Either way, this meant after living here for several months, we were moving again across the community to a house that had a freestanding small barn, a shop, and the house. It was on a small lot.

Amish Bread

The house itself had five bedrooms, four upstairs, one downstairs, a pantry, a kitchen, a living room, and a cellar to do laundry in. The kitchen was different than in the Amish communities where I had lived previously. They had kitchen cabinets with sinks in them. Our wasserbank was parked in a corner of the kitchen by the pantry, I found it quite different to be heating the water on the Pioneer Maid cookstove we had and washing dishes in the sink, instead of the wasserbank. This was really hoch (high/liberal). I punched my yeast bread dough carefully in the 13-quart stainless steel bowl as I thought about this. I decided, well I don't think making it easier to store things in the kitchen and clean up the kitchen is sinful. I flipped the dough as I was taught, lost in thought and then I screamed and jumped. Something that felt like a mouse had run over my foot. My heart pounded. What was that? Turns out our pet hamster had gotten out and run over my foot. My brother and mem came and helped me catch the hamster and put the hamster back in his tiny home. Then I washed my hands and finished my bread dough before I went to school. Whew! That was a narrow escape. I thought we had a mouse in the house, and I hate mice since sometimes my brothers would gang up to put mice on me and hold me there as they laughed at me.

I walked quickly to school, I was not going to arrive in time to do anything but get to my desk and start working, but this school was so bad. No one would play with me most of the time. At recess they would all get in their groups. The bishop's daughter would have consequences for anyone that dared talk to me. They would kick me out of whatever area I was in. My mem had encouraged me to have a sleepover with the bishop's daughter who was a year younger than me, this was an awful idea, and someone told her that I sometimes wet my bed still. I wet the bed regularly and I had wet the bed at during the sleepover at her house.

Then the bullying really began. The absolute worst day of my life at this age. I was unpopular and I was not liked nor cared about by anyone. Not even the teacher cared. Children alienated me and refused to play with me. It was so bad I couldn't even walk to and from school with anyone.

I quickened my stride as I walked to school, I didn't want to be late for school. I popped around the curve and was surprised to see the bishop's daughter with her cousin. I asked if I could walk with them, and they responded with some mean things. The bishops daughter said, "You can't walk with anyone." I said, "Who died and left you boss?" She said, "No one, who died and left you boss?" I said my dat. I cried the rest of the way to school after I passed them.

I was always alone because I chose to be alone rather than with cruel people. Then I would get in trouble for not being more like the rest of the girls and not playing with the others and there were notes sent home. If I got in trouble at school well there was double trouble at home.

This is the only community I ever saw people go in a van and vote on election day. I watched the driver pick up my mem and taking her to vote. She was gone a long time and I hid in the cellar the whole time until he brought her back. Our previous communities were not allowed to vote by die adning (the ordnung) so this was a remarkable experience to see that my mem could vote in an English election. It made an impact on me when I saw that women could vote.

One day when we were playing ball, some kids laughed at me as I ran after the ball. Little did I know there was barbed wire in the grass, and I tripped and fell on it tearing a hole in my leg. It took a long time to heal because it was deep, and it left a significant scar.

Test time for arithmetic. I carefully wrote all my answers and turned my test in. I noticed funny looks; I couldn't figure out what was going on in my mind. At recess, I had to speak with the teacher. She informed me that I was accused of cheating on my arithmetic test. I did not cheat. I never cheated on tests, but I got accused of cheating by a boy and the teacher believed it and I had to retake the test because a boy claimed I did. I DID NOT CHEAT.

Some of my classmates were troublemakers the adults said, when they put a large egg under the teachers buggy seat and left it there so long it rotted. If you know what a rotten egg smells like, imagine that in your buggy.

The other trick played on the teacher was untying the bell rope and attaching it to a bale of twine, so the teacher couldn't ring the bell for us to come in from recess. Of course, the teacher had a tug from a harness that she took into the basement with her to punish the transgressor, I heard the smacks and the child crying.

In this community on Fridays we would take bags of popcorn and other snacks to school instead of a regular lunch. We might have a sandwich or a cookie or something else with it. The popcorn was delicious and often seasoned with sour cream and onion or with cheddar cheese. Unfortunately, sometimes unruly children would throw popcorn everywhere and/or there were spills. On Friday afternoons, the girls would clean the schoolhouse and typically were assigned specific tasks, so it wasn't fair as we had to clean up the mess behind the boys, but this was part of submission. Obedience and the lords will, I thought.

Old Order Amish Two 1994-1996

Whirly Pop Popcorn maker and seasoning

I sat on the steps at the back of the school and watched the boys drag a girl into the boys outhouse. I cried as I grabbed a book. I knew I couldn't say anything, nobody cared anyways, what was the point? I read my book and tried not to think about it as I said "The Lord's Prayer" silently. Jarred from my thoughts and the book by my teacher sitting next to me.

Mary, you aren't even trying to talk to the other girls. I need you to talk with them at recess.

Me: si vella mich net. (They don't want me)

Teacher: well, you must try to be nicer to them.

Me: Ok.

The horrors didn't stop at school. They were still going on at home. I wasn't safe anywhere, so I started going into the small woods and trying to hide. Eventually I gave up. I started taking the straight pins during school and church, I would thread them through skin on the palm of my hand without drawing blood, over and over. This was a way of coping without really harming myself.

What's the point in trying to protect yourself from so much evil when no one cares about you—if they even notice your existence?

Besides that, I didn't have a dat so that made me unfit to play with according to the bishop's daughter. She was so cruel and mean to me and treated me like I was lower than the dirt everyone else walked on. I didn't understand and still don't. How can someone be so cruel to another person? One thing that I do understand is that cruelty is often taught. So, who taught her to be that cruel?

When I told my mem what was still happening to me everywhere including my bedroom and the outhouse, my mem said, "You should just be thankful you are not pregnant." When I started menstruation, I had no idea what was happening to me. My mem told me that I can have babies and I should make sure that doesn't happen. When my menstruation didn't come in 28 days as it should have, my mem made me a tea to drink. I drank it multiple times a day until menstruation began. This continued throughout the rest of my Amish community life. Today, I know this tea is an abortifacient, but I am grateful I was not forced to carry a rapists baby.

I listened to my rapist brother yell at my mem that she usually took me places with her. Tears ran down my cheeks. I was afraid of him. My mem and him eventually stopped fighting. The next time mem went somewhere, I was left at home, and I was downstairs washing the dishes like I was supposed to be as soon as I heard the buggy go. I RAN as fast as I could. This happened multiple times throughout the rest of my time in our Amish homes. I locked the door, but by the time I locked the door perpetrator #1 was climbing through the window. As he brutally assaulted me for what seemed like forever, I watched me become two people.

One part of me floated in the air and moved away and ran.

And ran.

And ran.

And when he unlocked the door and it clicked suddenly, I was one person again. I sobbed and sobbed. Why God?

Why did you not protect me?

I believed.

I promise I believed.

I cried out to God, I don't understand why are you punishing me. I've done everything. I wore my cap forward. I wore my dress chite (properly). I did everything I was supposed to. Why?

I still don't know what he did. I was gone.

Our old dog Laddie had moved with us, from house to house until he passed away. I missed my friend. He was a good friend to pet and be around. He always made me feel better.

I coughed and coughed. I was sick again. This time it was the whooping cough. I couldn't stop coughing. Nothing seemed to help—the sugar, butter and ginger mixture did not help. I felt like poop. I couldn't sleep because I was coughing so hard. Our mem made us all a cup of tea, with honey, ginger, lemon, and a shot of Seagram 7 in it before bed one night. I was disgusted by it and almost threw up.

When I finally recovered, I was glad to go back to school so I could have access to more books to read. As I was making my way through the entire school library, I read The Adventures of Huckleberry Finn, Tom Sawyer, Uncle Tom's Cabin, and the Anne of Green Gables series. Reading was a way to be transported beyond the world I lived in, to a place where struggle existed, but it was different from my struggle.

Clop, clop, clop, Colby's hooves were making a steady even sound as we pulled around the bend in our surrey. The neighbor's house came into view as we slowed. Our neighbor came out to the road to talk to our mem in the front seat, I was seated on the third bench and just waited in my own thoughts as they visited. Clop, clop, Colby was a spirited horse and eager to go so the surrey started with a lurch and off we were on our way to another widows home. I hoped I could be good enough to be friends with the widows daughters.

I was startled back to reality as the surrey went off the road and into the ditch. With a crash I entered nothingness, returned to reality again by my brother's screaming. I looked at his arm with his hand hanging at a grotesque angle. My mem took our brother to hospital. Afterward, we were still taken to the widow's home for supper. She was a kindly woman that gave me candy she had made. It was so good. My brothers arm was in a cast, and my mem and brother came too. I don't know that I was good enough to be friends with her girls though. It was weird.

There was a neighbor family that had a lot of sons and one daughter as well. One evening an Amish taxi driver backed over their young son who wasn't even two yet with their van. It was sad when I saw the little coffin.

I just wondered, was this baby the luckiest as the preacher preached? Would it be better not to have to live with all the things that have been done to me? Would it have been better if I died instead of this existence?

How can I kill myself?

Can I make it look like an accident?

Nobody would care or miss me; it would be just like this baby. The preachers words repeated in my head again: "This baby is so lucky, died before they can become sinful." I wished it were me. I looked for ways to die in my despair, I wasn't pure for my future husband I was expected to have. I thought about drinking gas, and I wondered if it would instantly kill me if I did. I did taste it, but I just couldn't get it down, so I gave up. I went to the back of the shop and played with the rabbits, except there was a rabbit missing and later we ate the rabbit for supper.

We had a woodpile behind the shop too, and one winter morning, there was a bobcat on the woodpile. It was good to see a bobcat, but we didn't want the bobcat this close to us.

There was a nice hill here to go sledding on the dirt road in the wintertime. Some children would come out with skis, others would go to the frozen over pond across the road from us and go ice skating. I couldn't ski and I couldn't ice skate, but I could ride my sleigh down the hill. It was a treat. Far too quickly, mem called us to go home for supper. This was a rare occasion, a Saturday, when we got to do this.

I remember when I was finally allowed to wear a fanna zu rok(front closing dress), closed with straight pins and a cape and apron along with wearing a white Kap at home. On church Sundays, unmarried girls would wear a black church kap instead of a white one. Under the age of 12, girls would wear a back closing dress with buttons and a different style of kap, and at night we would wear another style of kap to sleep in. To chore in, we would wear a kopduch, babies would wear a differently made covering too.

We were at my friends home. She and I both read the same books, Sweet Valley Twins. She had books in her closet inside the suitcase and we were looking through the books when I was horrified by her dad coming into her room, whispering to her. She then asked me to leave and come back in about 20 minutes. I was terrified for her and wondered if she too was experiencing the harm, even more so when I saw her crying when I came back. We bonded over books and read our books to help us cope with our lives. (For the record, this case was reported to law enforcement by an Amish person many years later, he was prosecuted and convicted of sexual crimes, but remains an Amish man in the church).

My mem had birds in a cage, a cockatiel, and two parakeets, Bobby and Betsy. I liked watching and handling them. They were so beautiful with their bright colors, sometimes I wondered why if color was sinful were birds, then given such beautiful colors? Bobby got out one day and we never saw him again. Betsy was a green parakeet, and she didn't do well without Bobby. I don't remember what happened to her or the cockatiel. Momentous changes were happening in my life and with my access to coping skills.

Remember Penny, the small chihuahua that slept with me? One day my mem told me the neighbors had Penny and she was biting everyone. I begged to got to the neighbors and see her. When I got to the neighbors, she was biting the neighbors. "Penny!" I called. She trembled in the corner and finally came and jumped in my arms. I don't know what happened to her at that house, but I begged my mem to bring her home and she finally said yes, I could have her back, I was so happy I got her back. Sometime later she hid under my brother bed and had a stillborn puppy, I didn't even know she was going to have puppies. She still slept with me and comforted me often.

In June 1996, my mem was announced by the bishop at church to be re-married to a widower from Wisconsin.

The wedding prep was a bustle and hustle, I remember it was a blur except the decorating of the wedding cakes. Watching that was a beautiful event where frosting became beautiful shapes and created designs that I found gorgeous.

After the wedding cakes were made, the tables were set, and everything was ready for the wedding. I watched as my aunt Hannah and uncle came and talked to my mem about this widower having a temper and being concerned for her. My mem said, "But what can I do? The wedding's been announced now, and the tables are set, everyone is here for the wedding. I can't call it off now. It's too late now." When I met soon to be stepfather, my skin crawled from the way he looked at me. I did not feel safe around him at all. When I begged my mem not to marry him, she said sadly "I made my bed, now I must lie in it."

Later, I cried alone in my room as I lay in bed, trying to sleep. I knew my life was changing forever with that man being my new stepfather and he terrified me. I had so many thoughts going round in my head:

What kind of world was I living in?

Was no one allowed to change their mind?

What kind of future would I have?

I felt so afraid of this man, my new stepfather. I cried and cried as I sucked my thumb as I finally drifted off to sleep only to be awakened by more night terrors.

One of my stepfather's first acts prior to the marriage was to get rid of Penny. My mem sent her to my aunt in another community to live. That puppy had been with me for a while in the previous community and then later she passed due to negligence. No one told me. No one would answer my questions about how Penny was doing. The horror I felt later as I read the letter finally was answering the question of what happened to Penny. My aunt gave me a beautiful cut glass blue lamp for Penny.

No object will ever replace the part Penny played in providing compassionate support for me as I struggled with staying alive. She was great to talk to, she was wonderful to pet and a puppy that just loved me, rather than denying my feelings, existence, or autonomy.

It was a long journey to reconcile the betrayal I felt from having to re-home her to a place where she was neglected, and she paid the ultimate price: her life.

Don't worry though, I obeyed my soon to be stepfather and my mem obeyed my soon to be stepfather. It was considered an act of submission to God's will, so there could be hope for my soul to go to heaven someday at the end of the world when Christ came, and every knee would bow to him. I would now have hope. My mem would have hope.

Dissecting this theology as an adult led me to understand that I was a child when this happened, I had no actual control over re-homing Penny to a negligent home.

Was it really my fault?

Was it the fault of the negligent people?

The conclusion I arrived at is this: like other areas of life, my mem was brainwashed to believe that she must do whatever the man in charge of her says. However, she still chose to marry this man and she chose to obey and submit to his guidance. My stepfather chose to exert this kind of control over my mem and her children and I know that she experienced domestic violence because I witnessed it.

She chose to continue putting me in dangerous situations as a child.

The plan was to move to Wisconsin after the wedding. How was that going to go? I was terrified of any of the possibilities by now,

The day of the wedding dawned, and I was startled back to reality where things were getting worse and there was no escape from it. I was glad I got to eat fried wedding chicken. I remember which corner of the house the Wedding Corner was and that's about it. Sadly, I survived it.

A lot of our things were sold, and other belongings were loaded on a truck hauling a trailer and moving several states away to my stepfather's community. My parents hired a van driver to take all of us to our new home.

What could be worse than what I just saw and experienced, I asked myself?

Today, I am in possession of information that causes me to view these experiences as something no child deserves or should experience. The alienation and terror I constantly felt was quite frankly awful. The spuhtting (mocking) and bullying from school age children was horrendous. It served to further alienate me from my peers. I was a misfit. I didn't meet the criteria to have friends. I was too different to be considered "good enough."

If you have ever experienced bullying and mocking, I want you to know this is not your fault. We are all human beings. We all deserve basic human rights which include safety. While everyone has differences that make them human, we also have similarities that make us the same. Being different than the socially accepted things isn't necessarily a bad thing and when we start celebrating our differences, we humanize one another.

Life would be boring if all of us were the same. We would never get to grow and learn new things. Some people are better at different things than other people and that's ok. While I am great at baking, my partner is better at cooking and quite frankly I hate cooking. It's beautiful because my partner cooks the most wonderful food for me. I get to make baked goods. It all balances out in the end.

When we collectively band together and lift our voices as one for the most basic human right for children, we will change the course for future generations of children and people in the world.

Chapter Four

Old Order Amish Three

1996-1998

"Do the best you can until you know better. Then when you know better, do better."

— *Maya Angelou*

We pulled up in the 15-passenger van to this home, a house with a dawdi house attached to it. In this dawdi house, there were four bedrooms, three upstairs and one downstairs, there was an open room half filled with storage items—this open room is where I slept—a kitchen, living room, basement, and an attached furniture shop. There were several sheds, a pig barn, and a dairy barn.

In this community, the youth drove around in open buggies, and they used oil lanterns on the buggies. The more boxy and wide pleated coverings were completely different from any of our previous communities, the dresses were made with pulled in folds on the bottom, the top was like our last community. The courtship rules were different too. This community did not allow smoking.

When everyone went inside, we were met by my stepbrother and his family that lived in the other part of the house, as well as my stepbrother who was disabled. It took a long time for me to feel ok here and I would say, I never really got there. My stepbrother and his family were a bit difficult for me to talk to. It seemed like everything I did was wrong to them, and they complained about it to my stepfather and then I'd either get a talking to or hit with items within reach and I never knew which was coming.

I woke up startled awake, I thought I heard a noise and now I had wet my bed again. I got up and changed. I cried as I tried to go back to sleep, and then I heard another noise, and sure enough next thing I know, I was being sexually abused again in my bed. When he left, I just sobbed silently to myself. What is wrong with me? Why? Why will no one help me?

I still couldn't go to the outhouse without an intense fear of being raped. After I told my mem the last time a different rapist spent two hours chasing me until they finally caught me, it was one of the most horrific experiences of all of them, I thought I finally got away from him. NO, I did not.

Where was God?

I would wonder, was I thin enough?

Did I eat enough?

Did I eat too much?

I couldn't make my white schatz (apron) stay unwrinkled in church.

Was it my shape?

Was it me?

Why?

I cried because it never worked.

In church, the sadness was overwhelming as I carefully watched and copied every single action of the girls who did not wrinkle their schatz but it wrinkled my schatz anyway. As I transitioned into a woman shaped body, it became curvy. I near starved myself as I hated having those curves and they added to the inability to conform. I'd feel guilty for eating. When I ate, I'd go to the outhouse and make myself throw up, because I didn't deserve to eat, and my body didn't conform. I had wide hips and people would make comments about how small my schatzbandle (apron string) was around the waist in comparison.

At the same time, I was being violated. Repeatedly and when I asked for help.

The icing on the cake was again being told by mem to "just be glad you're not having a baby" and you're not praying hard enough or believing hard enough.

Excuse me: you're telling your 12–14-year-old child to be glad she's not pregnant. (And pregnant by a rapist because that would be harder to keep silent than just silencing the victim of abuse without a "baby" as evidence).

At this point I already had a ton of scars decorating my body, scars that were well hidden by my clothing. I had disfigurement in my private body parts caused by an especially brutal CSA where I was tortured.

My body betrayed me because it was inciting people to lust after me and that made it my fault when they raped me.

I wanted to fix it.

I wanted to die. I prayed to die.

Wouldn't the kindest thing have been for God to let me die at that point?

I tried to die, I begged to die. Why would anyone want to live in this existence, where laughing too loud is a sin and people raping you is your fault?

I hated myself and my life. I prayed to be relieved of that misery; yet NOTHING changed. My dearly beloved mem again said it must be my fault because I wasn't praying hard enough, and I must want these things to happen because they keep happening. I tried to die. I prayed to die every night and truly if God is such a merciful and just God, what was the purpose in looking down at this little child forced to live a life that was worse than nonexistence? I started questioning everything in my mind about religion, I read everything I could from the school library and read the Bible. I had the impression even as a child that I should be careful in reading the Bible as it can be faführish (misleading).

I swung my lunchbox as I made my 2-mile trek to school. I was so afraid. Again, I was going to my fifth school, and I was in seventh grade. Only two more years I told myself and then I would never have to go back. My mem had said that school was a waste of time, and I could be helping at home more. Strangely enough, I got in trouble soon for not getting good enough grades from my stepfather. It was clear there was a disagreement on this.

I dreaded meeting the new classmates. I was never going to fit in well. It was a pleasant surprise to be the only other person in my grade and to also make friends with a neighbors girl that walked to school and home with me often. I had a whole new school library to choose books from and I read all of them after I finished my schoolwork.

Drawing I made inspired by my uncle

I remember being a small child and going with my mem to my uncle and aunts house. My uncle took me fishing in the pond and we caught a fish. It was a beautiful experience. Later my uncle took a piece of paper and a pen and drew a bird on a log for me. I loved it. I didn't understand when I heard people say my uncle was so bad, they said he was " nervich" (nerve problems) and bipolar. He never did anything to me, and I loved spending time with him. He was kind to me at a time when few people were. So, as I was now 13 years old and I couldn't sleep,

I thought of this, and I drew this bird in my Neues (New) Testament. It didn't come out how I wanted it to, so I scribbled over it and colored over it. I missed my uncle and I wanted to go back to that state and spend time with my uncle again, but I knew that was unlikely to happen and I cried myself to sleep.

September was already here, and I was at school again. One day I walked home with my brothers and the house was weird. Our stepfather came out of the bedroom and told me to go to the neighbors, so I turned around and backtracked to our neighbors house. I got to chore with my friend from the school that was a little older than me. It was nice. Soon though, someone told me to come home again, I did and when I came home, mem was in bed with a baby, my sister. She was tiny and perfect. I loved her from the moment I met her. I didn't want to go to school if I could hold her. Mem's earlier words about holding babies spoiling them kept running through my head. Our neighbor's daughter came over to maud schaffa (work as a hired maid).

The Shawl Pin I used to pin my shawl

Crunch, crunch my shoes went as I walked the two miles to school. Winter was here, and it was cold. I bundled up in my coat, kopduch, kapp, scarf, ivakapp (winter bonnet) shawl and gloves but my ears were still cold and hurt. Once I got to school, I set my lunchbox on the shelf and unbundled my winter clothes. The schoolhouse was cozy warm with the woodstove going and I stood next to it, to warm up. All too soon it was time to start our school day. We had two periods each morning and two periods each afternoon. At the end of the day, we sang the same song everyday "Ich Sage Gut Nacht." (I tell you, Good Night)

O Gott Vater, wir loben dich, (Oh Lord Father, we praise you)

Und deine gute preisen. (And your goodness praise)

We sang this song every morning to start our school day and we also said The Lord's Prayer in HochDeutsch. I dreaded singing "Ich Sage Gut Nacht" on freezing days like this, because then we'd have to walk home in the cold, and hurry, because it was time for evening chores.

One day at recess, we went sledding on the hill in the pasture behind the schoolhouse. As I walked back up, Edwin told me, "Mary, I like you." I said "Edwin, I don't like you" and quickened my pace so I wouldn't have to talk to him. The next day, I got in so much trouble from mem and stepfather because I made him cry. My mem told me this is wrong, and you must go apologize to him.

Reluctantly, I approached him at school and said "I'm sorry I hurt your feelings," because I knew if I didn't, they'd attempt to break my will, again. I didn't like him like that. In fact he made my skin crawl, and *I liked a girl*, but I couldn't talk about that. I learned my lesson very well about how I couldn't talk about liking girls.

There was no one in our community, family, or home I could talk to about the way I felt and how the ministers preached against it and how I was tortured, and it started with me saying *I wanted to marry a woman*. I wondered if I was being punished for wanting to marry a woman and this was me suffering for Jesus, after all the sermons I heard often said it was better to suffer on earth than have an easy life and not make it to Heaven.

In the fall, the maple forest was great. I liked to see the leaves become colorful. I walked through the woods alone and hid in a tree. It was nice, no one ever found me there.

In the springtime, I walked into the shack with the steam rolling out of it. It was maple syrup making time and I was bringing something to my stepfather. I hoped I was good enough so that he would let me have a glass of warm maple syrup to drink. It was one of the best things in the world. Today was a wonderful day, I got to stir the fire under the vat where the sap was boiling and add more wood. Then I got a small glass of warm syrup to drink before I rushed back to the house to help my mem.

I went to the last day of school and got my eighth-grade diploma with my name on it. On one hand, I was glad I didn't have to be around Edwin anymore. On the other hand, I loved reading, and I was sad to stop learning things. It was a day of mixed feelings and life as I knew it was changing.

By now my stepbrother and family had long moved out of their side of the house and the whole house was now inhabited by us. This added more bedrooms, and I finally got my own room again. Safety wise nothing changed, I was still unsafe in my home and my own bedroom. I hated living and I wished to die.

I swung the hoe vigorously. I was so hot, tired, and I was out hoeing the garden again. I loved eating fresh peas and corn on the cob but the rest of it, meh. We had rhubarb, blackberry, raspberry, and rose bushes. I loved the rose bushes and I cut a rose off and dried it. I had it for a long time.

My mem had taught me to can food and I was busy all summer long, canning food, making jam, cutting the grass with a push lawnmower (this was a big yard, and it took several hours), burning the trash on the other side of the road, cleaning, doing the laundry and hanging it outside, mending, sewing clothing, ironing, and other chores my mem assigned me.

Since I was still wetting my bed, my mem frequently would hire a driver to take me to another Amish community to see an Amish chiropractor and I would get adjustments from it. It didn't help, but when we heard rumors that he might be inappropriate with women, we never went back again. But I still had no help that resulted in me not wetting my bed or having night terrors or trouble falling asleep. I must ask, since most

Amish only go to eighth grade what qualified him to be a chiropractor?

I found some solace watching the sun rise and set. "Mary!" Mem called, "Where are you?" Jolted back to the present I ran back to the kitchen and helped with breakfast. "Where were you?" Mem fussed at me. I had to go to the outhouse, I said. I sighed. There never seemed to be enough time to get everything done.

I hid books and read them every chance I got. Books were my escape from the terror and horror that I experienced as I watched my stepfather become increasingly violent. The day I saw him grab a stove poker in the living room and strike one of my brothers with it. I freaked. I couldn't breathe as my heart pounded. I knew better than to make a sound. I made myself as small as possible and tried to stay out of sight. This opened my eyes to what kind of a person my stepfather was, and it was not a good impression.

One of my abusers was getting married. The wedding day was a blur, in part I felt relief because I wouldn't see him all the time, while that helped remove direct access, it did not entirely remove his access. He and his new wife visited us, and we would visit them.

The sexual abuse did not just stop because suddenly one person was gone who had facilitated so much harm to so many children. It continued. When I went to the basement to grab peaches, ground beef and canned peas to cook for supper, someone was waiting to hurt me. There was no escape.

I told my mem who did what. She told my stepfather who then beat him to break his will. It happened again. I felt faced with an impossible task of trying to prevent my abusers from raping me.

It wasn't just the people waiting to hurt me that were beaten to break their will. I felt even more fear of my stepfather when I saw my him going in the cellar while another brother was taking his weekly bath. We only took baths once a week. Water was heated in the big iron kettle over a wood fire to take a bath in the cellar. I heard a big ruckus that I don't have words for. I couldn't make sense of it. My brother was old enough to wash himself I thought, he'd been doing it for years. I was even more afraid of my stepfather. I didn't know what to make of this back then and even now this doesn't make any sense, but it replays in my head frequently as I go about my life.

One of my brothers got extremely sick and had a fever over 103. I watched my mem take care of him and she had me make him tea and bring him food. My stepfather called a local doctor (an actual board-certified medical doctor) to come out to the house to see him. I kind of hoped he would die, since he was one of the people who hurt me, but the doctor prescribed medicine that helped and before long he was back to normal.

One day I'm in the kitchen helping my mem.

Mem: "Du muszt dich chite aw shikka." (Behave yourself)

Me: "Was mainst du?" (What do you mean?)

Mem: Da dat hat dich uch si shoz hocka ghat. Du bist zu alt fa uch da dat si shoz hocka. Du vit net havva es ehr di letzi ideas grickt. Du michst act geva wan man's leit do rum sin, sie hen so viel lust and du whilst nets matcha es sie faila ams lust fechta. Mansleut sin net wie weibsleut, si kenna nets lust grad fechta.

(Your dad had you sit on his lap. You are too old to sit on his lap. You don't want him to get the wrong ideas. You must be careful when men are around, they have so much lust and you don't want to make it, so they fail at fighting their lust. Men are not like women; they cannot fight lust right away.)

Immediately, I had a Flashback: "Mary," my stepfather had called, "come here." I went cautiously and quietly. I hoped he was in a good mood instead of a beating mood. He had a smirk on his face as he told me you are a schone maedel (beautiful girl) and then beckoned me to come closer and said: "Do you want to sit on my lap?"

And he too joined the club of touching me inappropriately in private areas.

I felt dirty afterwards. It confused me because it didn't hurt the same way I had already been hurt. Then he let me go.

Does mem think I wanted that? I thought to myself. " I wondered if she thought I was competing for my stepfather's attention. Am I behaving immodestly, I asked myself?

What am I doing wrong?

Why ?

Rice Crispies

I stirred the grated chocolate carefully in the double boiler to melt it. I was so happy we were making chocolate covered cherries for Christmas. I carefully dipped them and placed them on wax paper. My mem, my brother Moses and I had already made a gallon of turtles, rice crispy treats, peanut brittle, and more types of candy. It was amazing to be ready for Christmas and have all this candy. I loved making candy with them. We also baked cookies for Christmas. It was the one time a year we brought out the cookie press and made some of my favorite cookies, the butter spritz cookies. But I had to hurry as I made them because wasting time was considered faul (lazy) and no one wants a lazy wife is what I was told over and over. Regardless, baking cookies and making candy is still one of my favorite things to do, especially with people I love.

After two years at this house, my parents decided to sell the farm and move to another community. I already knew I was going to miss the views here, the sugar maples, the berries, the mailbox with the flowers around it. It always just looked so pretty.

I don't know why specifically we moved. I know there was discourse in the community and conversations about people not getting along, but I have no idea why we moved away from here. Moving day dawned and a driver with a truck and trailer came as well as Amish people and we loaded it all up and took off to our new home. As always, I hoped that in the new community there would be a fresh start, and no one would be mean or abusive.

You can move, but you sure can't escape yourself or your abusers when they move with you. Sometimes to navigate life, we must face the issue and go through it instead of running from it, denying that it happens or pretending things aren't happening.

When we minimize what was done to us, we tell ourselves we are not worth emotions, effort, or even healthy relationships. We are worthy of love that isn't contingent upon us meeting the persons needs to receive love.

Let me explain what a survivor is according to the Sexual Assault Kit Initiative:

"A victim is someone who has had a crime committed against them, often used as a legal term in the justice system"

"A survivor is someone who experienced a crime and has begun the healing process, it may empower the person to continue healing or even begin healing by saying survivor instead of victim"

We have survived unbearable trauma that causes us to have effects of night terrors, triggers, flashbacks, insomnia, memory problems, medical problems but we are nothing less than perfectly imperfect!

Despite *ALL THAT* many of us lead happy lives and feel productive in our lives.

We contribute to doing things we find meaningful and healthy for us.

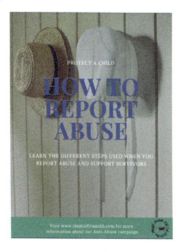

https://www.themisfitamish.com/amishresources

For example, look at the brochures a group of survivors made in collaboration with psychologist's, detectives, and an editor!

Some survivors create organizations for meaningful change!

Some survivors write, record and video record their stories for meaningful change!

Some survivors network with people to change laws (think Erin's law).

Some survivors build professional relationships, with ethical values and collaborating within those values.

Some survivors navigate life to the best of their ability as they are unable to speak, write, record, or even discuss what happened to them openly. (This is ok!)

Survivors are amazing!

We have faced so much fear in life, we know how to live life facing fear and still despite it all take definitive action.

Education is prevention and prevention is key.

Nothing... Is better than those who walk through hell getting out carrying buckets of water to douse the fires for those who come behind them.

Chapter Five

Old Order Amish Four

1998-2004

"Silence creates its own violence."

— *Jeff VanderMeer, Annihilation*

Buggies

We moved to a whole new community that was so much smaller. I was glad I already completed school, so I didn't attend school here. It was a whole new world, we had battery lights on our buggies and closed buggies for everyone. I remember the marvel of the men having chainsaws here was a miracle. My brother put an engine on a baler, and we baled some hay. We put other hay loose with a fork in the haymow.

Men dressed similar to the previous communities' rules, with their clothing sewn by their mothers, wives, or sisters. Women and girls, however, did not wear the wide pleated box kapp. Kappa were to be finely pleated and pulled in folds along the side. We were now allowed to use a barrette to hold our hair together to put it up along with the hair pins that often dug into our scalp, but I really appreciated the barrette instead of yarn tying my hair together. In several of my previous Amish communities, women and girls wearing a front closing dress had taken a piece of yarn and tied it over their hair and around their chin, then used pins to pin their hair up, and finally untied the yarn, pulled it tight and put it up too. I liked putting the new folds in the bottom of the dress as they were folded in, instead of pulled in folds on the bottom. We ironed those folds flat. Our dresses could be eight inches from the floor. We could have sinks in our counters with cold running water. We had harmonicas and I received one as a gift.

This house had the most bedrooms of all the houses I ever lived in, eight bedrooms, seven upstairs and one downstairs. There was a cellar and an attic too. On Saturdays I did most of the cleaning and Moses would help me do laundry, cook, and clean. He often washed dishes for us all. He was a leather worker too and hand carved leather billfolds, belts and more. I loved watching him work magic on leather.

Hand carved leather wallet

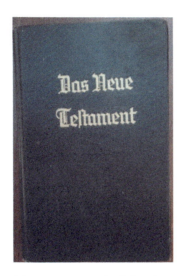

Since I was not in school, I was expected to work all the time except Sundays. I was always glad when it was an in between Sunday and I relaxed by reading the Bible. I gasped as I read Romans 13:1-4:

*Transcribed from Das Neue Testament, D Martin Luther, reprinted in 1991 for Raber's Bookstore, Baltic Ohio, translated in 1914 for Berlin for The Bible Society.

"Jedermann sei unterthan der obrigkeit, die gewalt uber ihn hat. Denn ist keine obrigkeit, ohne von Gott; wo aber obrigkeit ist, die ist von Gott verordnet.

Wer sich nun wider die Obrigkeit Setzet, der widerstrebet Gottes Ordnung; die aber widerstreben, warden uber sich ein Uhrteil emphangen.

Denn die Gewaltigen sind nicht den guten werken, sondern den bosen zu furchten vor den Obrigkeit. Willst du dich aber nicht zu furchten vor die Obrigkeit, so thue Gutes, so wirst du lob von derselben haben."

(Everyone is subject to the authority that has violence over him. For there is no obligation without God; but where there is obligation, it is ordained by God.

Whoever opposes authority now opposes God's order; but those who resist will receive a part of the clock.

Because the powerful are not the good works, but the evil to fear from the authorities. But if you don't want to be afraid of the authorities, then do good, and you will have praise from them.)

I jumped up and headed downstairs to ask my mem about this, mem told me to ask my stepfather. I carefully approached my stepfather and waited for his acknowledgement. He asked me what I wanted, and I said it says here we don't have to be afraid of the government if we are doing good things. Also, if the government is appointed by God, doesn't that mean God is looking out for us?

Shouldn't we really submit to the government too? So why do we talk about the government coming to take Amish children? Why do the preaching's also say that? I watched as my stepfather made a face and carefully answered "Man was created first, woman was created second, from his rib. A woman or girl could never comprehend this passage right. The ministry is chosen by God. They know better what that means, just listen to them."

We had days assigned to do things like wash on Monday, and it was a race to see which woman could get their laundry out the earliest. My brother Moses, who had a disability would work in the house with me. I felt like I knew him the best out of all my siblings. He was often mocked by various children after church for his seizures as well as because he was different. Even adults talked negatively about him. My stepfather was not kind to him at all. My brother though, was one of the kindest people I have ever known. He showed me so much love, compassion, acceptance, and empathy.

My mem also taught me to sew our plain dresses and fix our kappa. It would take me around an hour to "petz (pinch) a kapp." The starch had to be right, and I would carefully light the gasoline iron we used. I was glad we had a gasoline iron instead of the irons you put on the wood stove to heat them up. It was harder to iron the way I should with those irons as the temperature of the iron was unreliable. Ironing all the Sunday clothes was always a requirement and there were eleven humans who needed Sunday clothes prepared for them.

When I learned to sew men's Sunday suits, men were measured specifically and made appropriately for them in di adning (the ordnung according to church rules), not too tight and not too loose. Specifically, the baptized men wore mutza suits with a slit tail in the back and unbaptized boys wore a coat without the split tail in their suit. Sewing in the split was one of the most frustrating things to learn to do, I was so proud when I accomplished it.

It was good to finally be able to sew independently. I sang as I sewed, "Mary took to running with a traveling man, she left her mama crying with her head in hands" ("Leaving Louisiana in Broad Daylight," by The Oak Ridge Boys). I heard someone coming so I stopped immediately and switched to humming. I knew if I was caught, I would be in big trouble. I was making my baptism dress. I hoped it would be perfect with the one ¼ inch belt and perfectly spaced folda (folds in the back of the dress skirt), I didn't want it too tight on top as it felt like I couldn't breathe or move if it was too tight. The dresses had to be eight inches from the ground and the aprons and capes had to be made correctly too.

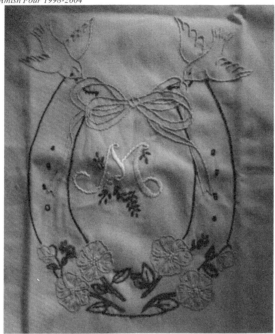

Embroidery sewing was not discouraged so when I was fifteen, I decided to embroider a design on my pillowcases by hand. It ended up being beautiful and I loved the way it came out, but this was so time-consuming. After these pillowcases were done, I don't think I ever completed another embroidery design. Productivity based value can lead you down strange paths such as never doing something you enjoyed and found great satisfaction in creating.

Besides, my mem was not happy with how long it took me to embroider those pillowcases and she told me multiples times to hurry up and finish them. It could be a combination of the judgement for not being as fast as someone else expected of me as well as the productivity-based value. I asked myself, "is my art really a waste of time? At that time, it felt like it was a waste of time since I had yet again failed to live up to the expectations of my mem. It devastated me.

Quilt I made with my mem

"But why can't we have other colors," I asked my mem? We were picking out colors to make quilts and I longed desperately to have color approved for our new quilts. I thought to myself, we make colorful quilts for English, why can't we make them for ourselves? I don't remember what my mem said, but it was enough that I felt despair at the thought that we would never have color. I continued cutting out the blocks per her instructions as she sewed the blocks together.

We sang together as we worked. It was quite pleasant to make an Ohio Star quilt together and we hand quilted it. It took us a long time to quilt it, but it was a great activity for the winter months. This quilt was on my bed in my room. We made and quilted quilts for my brothers beds as well. I was glad I had warm bedding in the winter, but it still destroyed me inside when I still despite it all, persisted in wetting my bed.

My mem gave me Secret brand deodorant and instructed me to use it before I go anywhere and when I get dressed in the morning.

It was Saturday night, and I was in the basement taking a bath. It was cold down there, I wanted to go to bed and smell good on Sunday morning when I went to church, so I scrubbed myself clean. Too bad I couldn't wash myself on the day of church. Sunday was a day of rest, except for chores, cooking meals, (but no baking) visiting and washing dishes. Sunday morning getting ready for church, I carefully sprayed my body spray on and spread deodorant so I wouldn't stink during church. I was so glad I had powder fresh deodorant and body spray to use so I wouldn't stink like the boys as it often got hot during church and my armpits would be sweaty and stinky like they were before I had deodorant. I pulled on my unnneruck (underdress), and my dress and I pinned it together. I hated the pins; my chest had a spot that was sore, and I finally looked at it. I had a three-inch spot that was bleeding. I put a bandage on it and pinned my dress on. I slowly pinned my apron on too. (We did not wear halsdicha (capes) during the week at home, if we went somewhere, we were more apt to put on a haslduch (cape) during the week). At least I smelled powdery fresh as I suffered for Jesus.

I never understood why, if the cape was how da gut mann (the good man/slang for God) wanted us to submit to his will, then why was his will only for the halsduch to be worn only on Sundays or when you went somewhere or had formal events to attend like a wedding or a quilting. The logic didn't make sense to me, but I didn't talk about it, because I didn't want to lose the privilege of going without my halsduch at home. (Little girls in all these communities didn't wear halsdicha at all, they only wore aprons everywhere).

Oh boy I had lost track of time again, Mem sounded upset as she called for me. I ran downstairs as fast as I could to start the day. As soon as I got downstairs, mem said that to obey and submit means to get up on time and come the first time she calls me (I had not heard her call me at all—this happened frequently throughout my childhood). I hung my head. I had failed again, I wondered why it was so hard for me to obey and hear her. I prayed that God would give me the ears to hear her every time she called me. She continued walking to me and the next thing I heard was, "I wish you were a boy, because boys are so much easier." I cried as I ran to the barn to start milking.

The chores were a part of earning my keep. Some people believe children should earn their keep or even owe their parents for giving them life. If I earned money, my parents kept it until I was twenty-one, just like they did with money my brothers earned. So, I knew if I wasted time, I wasn't worth anything since I wasn't earning my keep and milking cows was part of earning money since we shipped the milk to the cheese factory.

We had dairy cows to milk by hand, twice a day. It was critical to milk cows 12 hours apart and be on time. Our milkhouse was a small cement room with a tub for water that we would fill with cold water and put the 10-gallon milk cans in to keep them cool until the milk truck came to pick them up and truck them to a nearby Cheese Factory, owned by Amish. Because the milk was not put in a tank, it was all grade B milk.

Sometimes if a cow had an illness, the veterinarian had to be called to come out and if they treated them with meds, we would dump the milk. The milk would sometimes have straw, dirt etc. in it. It was important to strain it before consumption. And if someone forgot and put the milk through the strainer, we'd have to dump the entire ten gallon can of milk.

I'd sit beside Rita, one of our cows milking as gently and quickly as possible. She was a nervous cow and did not let most people milk her without kicking. I loved her. I'd pat her and talk to her before and after milking. She was a fan of gentleness.

After I milked my four cows, I headed to the house to cook breakfast for everyone with my mem and my brother Moses. We would most often make fried potatoes and gravy with sausage for breakfast. It was a rare treat to make pancakes for breakfast. We'd also make fried cornmeal mush with sausage for breakfast depending on the season. I always loved having maple syrup poured over the fried cornmeal mush. Other times we would cook a big pot of oatmeal and eat it with brown sugar and milk. As mem said though, oatmeal doesn't fill up growing boys.

My Bureau 1

Shelf above my bureau 1

    I took pride in my room. I carefully washed the towel on top of the bureau and the nightstand my stepfather finally made me. They were beautiful and I loved them so much. I washed the cut glass dishes I set carefully on top of the towel and the beautiful blue lamp on my nightstand until it all sparkled. The quilt on my bed that I quilted with my mem was beautiful and matched the blue tones of almost everything in my room. I had a cookie from being a table waiter at someone's wedding on a shelf above the bureau. It was a work of art to display every piece right and display greeting cards. I treasured the greeting cards that people would send me in the mail and often wrote letters with them. Writing back to people was hard though. It seemed like there was never enough time and I was working from before dawn till after dark and then it was bedtime. Every morning and evening we would all gather around the living room and kneel as our stepfather would lead us in prayer with a prayer from a church and parent approved prayer book, when he wasn't around my mem led us in prayer until my brothers were old enough to lead in prayer.

Thank you, card, displayed on my dresser 1

I heard the paper rip as I unwrapped the Christmas present from my parents. I hoped it was that nice blue dress material I had been eyeing for months. My heart fell as I realized it was a deep almost purple dress. It was preached in church that we shouldn't wear purple. It was the color Jezebel wore before she was thrown from the window and the dogs ate everything of her except her hands. It was horrifying to consider wearing a Jezebel color. I was already being terrorized unbelievably. What else would I invite them to do to me by making and wearing this dress?

I listened to the tea kettle whistle as I carried a 5-gallon bucket filled with water and dumped it in the reservoir on our pioneer maid stove. I loved the way it whistled and how the water made sounds while the fire crackled and heated it up. There was a big reservoir on this stove, and it took a couple buckets of water, but this is how we heated our water to wash our dishes. Thank goodness we had a water pump in the kitchen and a faucet over the sink where we washed dishes. I was no longer relegated by the church ministry to using a wasserbank to wash dishes here and I appreciated it. There were always so many dishes. It would take about 45 minutes to an hour for me to put away the food and wash dishes.

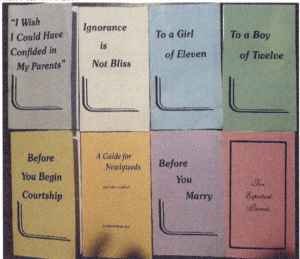

The Sacred Subjects, Pathway Publishers, Unidentified Amish Minister Author

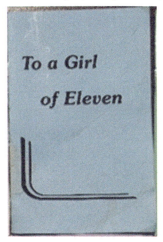

I'm standing in my mem and stepfathers bedroom with my mem in front of the bureau. I've told her yet again I'm being raped when I'm asleep.

I watch as she opens the second half drawer from the top, on the left and pulls out a stack of booklets, The Sacred Subjects. She said, "You must pray, have more faith and fight when they come for you." In despair, "I said but I did fight." She said, "You must fight harder and don't laugh and talk too much with boys and men." She handed me the booklet titled "To a Girl of Eleven." Just writing this today is upsetting my stomach. I can't begin to describe the horror and prayers I made so God could forgive me for not being a virgin, or as I read that it was my fault that I in fact enticed my brothers to lust after me. I collapsed into a sobbing heap and begged for my life to end.

The amount of despair at being told men in the world really are the ones to be afraid of meant there was no safety anywhere. If Amish men think it's my fault and I should be raped in my sleep, what are English men going to do?

I just wanted to die. I asked God to take my life and let me be. I didn't want to be like the girl my age that had a baby with her brother. The shame I felt in my bones had no end. The horror at the fact that no one had any help for me. My entire being was crushed and I was also told I was lazy and nervich (nervous/mental problems) for lying in bed, sleeping, and crying. My mem said men don't want a fauili frau (a lazy wife).

I simply couldn't get up some days, my mem would yell at me up the stairs, I would say I'm sick. It felt like I was sick. The crippling and debilitating depression I was living with, was eating me alive. This was a struggle the rest of my Amish life.

I knew I would get in trouble for it, I just couldn't get up. There was nowhere left for me to go for help. When I finally mustered up the energy to get out of bed AND WALK DOWNSTAIRS.

When I got to the bottom of the stairs, I was met by my stepfather who beat and choked me unconscious.

Although I had told yet again, that I was being raped. I learned my lesson after this and tried hard not to say a word about it, for what happened next was horrific and the abuse escalated.

By age 14 all my teeth except my wisdom teeth had been pulled by various dentists. When they pulled four teeth at once, my stepfather laughed and said, "Maybe that'll shut you up."

Right after I turned fifteen, we got in the van and the English driver drove to another state to Barbara Kiem's home, she was an Amish woman with an eighth-grade education making dentures in her kitchen. I then had to go back in three months to get the dentures. I was grateful my mouth wasn't flat anymore.

When my wisdom teeth hurt, they took me to an Amish dentist in the community, Joseph Yoder, who was doing this with an eighth-grade education, and injected cow novacaine into me in his chair in the living room. I felt the teeth coming out from the roots and was miserable. For the next 10+ years I had shards of teeth or what appeared to be bones coming out of my gums. Reminder Amish 8th grade education does not include any form of anatomy and physiology, let alone medical school information.

One of the highlights of my teenage life was getting to go to New York to my cousin's wedding. We got to my aunt's house—in the Amish communities I lived in, it is customary for the wedding feast to be at the bride's parents' house—before the wedding and it was so good to see my cousin Sarah. She was only a little older than me and we reconnected with each other by working together and having fun doing it as we prepared for her sister to get married. We got fussed at for horsing around too much as we completed tasks. Finally, the tables were set, the food was prepped, and the house was ready the night before the wedding. Off to bed we went.

The day of the wedding the house was filled with an air of expectancy. Everyone bustled around doing the tasks we were assigned to do. People invited to the wedding went to the neighbor's place where the ceremony would be performed. Often, the bride's mother oversees the cooking. Women and girls that were invited to be cooks and table waiters arrived early, the cooks completed the cooking, the table waiters prepped the tables and then most went off the watch the marriage. After the ceremony, while everyone else was still at church they returned, the table waiters and the cooks bustled around putting the final additions on the table with an Amish feast complete with dessert. Fried wedding chicken is delicious and amazing. It's one of my favorite foods.

After lunch, the bride and groom headed up to the brides' room to open presents with their side sitters. It is customary in all the Amish communities I have visited and lived in to have side sitters, two couples that would sit with the bride and groom on their wedding day. They had duties to perform, like signing the marriage license. The side sitters were chosen by the bride and groom; the bride chose one couple for her side, and the groom chose one for his side. Often, the bride or groom would ask one of their siblings to be one of the side sitters, and the sibling would want their partner to be the second person in the couple. The bride and groom would agree or disagree to that, but then they had to ask the selected person to be a side sitter with the person who chose them. It was always interesting to know who the side sitters were. The married folks would visit, and the young folks would visit too, much of the wedding was separated by men and women, boys, and girls as is typical for many Old Order Amish communities. The co-mingling for the young folks would happen later after supper. When it got to be close to chore time, people left to go complete their chores before supper. Of course, since we had traveled across several states to come to this wedding, we did not leave to do chores.

When people came back, supper was served and then more visiting was done by the married folks. I watched as the young folks here sang songs like "Skip, Skip, Skip to my Lou" while they skipped around. I saw two boys approach my cousin Sarah. She went off to talk with them and then joined the young folks skipping around. Eventually, the young folks went in a room to play a game, in a barn while the older men supervised them. (I did not watch this and had no desire to participate).

This community had different practices from our community, especially with the wedding, for one thing, if you were sixteen you probably were old enough to go with the young folks.

My momi passed away, I didn't go to her funeral, but I sure missed her. I have a postcard she gave me one time and it always reminds me to stand up to bullies. I missed her so much already through the years since I hadn't seen her in years, but I always knew she was there. She represented something good to me. Her character stood up to bullying in her life. She was a strong Amish woman who spoke her mind. I wanted to be like her in many ways.

Approximately, April 15th, 2002, I spent six hours that day trying to get away from a perpetrator of abuse and still was brutally thrown against the wall and hurt. There was no safety, there was no sanctuary, there was nowhere for me to go for help. I reached out to who I thought was my safe person and I was wrong. She did not help me; she didn't keep me safe. This woman told me I did NOT pray hard enough and that's why I was continually raped. My prayers were "LET me DIE so I can escape this hell I live in." God did not answer my prayers. Did God care about me, I asked myself?

The sermons on Sunday seemed to assure me that suffering for Jesus was the answer. In desperation I undertook the task of reading the Bible in its entirety again, it was an eye-opening experience for me. I had even more questions and wondered, what makes it so only men can grasp the meaning of the stories in the Bible?

My stepfather would have violent outbursts and hurt all of us. It really wasn't ok. When my stepbrother with a disability fell sick, he wouldn't call a doctor (nor would he allow anyone else to call a doctor) to come make him comfortable. And when my brother was so weak, his face was hollowed and sunken, and he couldn't sit up and eat. I watched in disbelief as my stepfather grabbed him by his shirt around the collar and hit him in the face with a closed fist. When my stepbrother passed away several days later, I was grateful that my stepfather couldn't hurt him anymore. No matter how much I miss my stepbrother, no one deserves to be treated like that. The grief over how he was treated is a bottomless well of endless sorrow that comes out in waves over time. My stepbrother did not deserve to be treated this way.

My brothers gravestone 1

Playing Dutch Blitz 1

Some in-between Sundays and even sometimes after church on Sundays, us children would play card games and board games like Dutch Blitz or battleship. My brother Moses would often sit at the table and put together puzzles. These are my most deeply treasured memories and I still enjoy a variety of board games with my loved ones. One game I remember playing was "I Doubt It," I am a terrible liar, I always have been. It took a ton of energy to play it and pretend not to be lying about the number, I was always exhausted after that game. After I was seventeen, I was old enough to be by di youngie leit (with the young folks). There were young folks get togethers at times that included alcohol being passed around. We would also play our auto valve harmonicas sometimes together after church. I loved it so much. I got in trouble for playing mine too much at home.

I was at an English hospital. The guy at the window asked for my photo with my name on it, my mem had told me prior to arrival to tell them, "I am Amish, we don't have those things, it's against our religion." I was here to visit my stepfather. He was sick and needed triple bypass surgery. I wasn't sure what that meant, but I didn't want to be here. I had watched before this as he refused to have Moses take Dilantin because it was too expensive. But we spent money on a battery-operated machine with leads attached to it, that would supposedly cleanse his body of all toxins and heal his seizures. Wonder of all wonders, it didn't heal his seizures from the spinal cord damage and that was just the Lord's Will. All I hear right now is my mem's voice es ist da hah si villa (It's the Good Mans will) (Good man is slang for God)."

I took a deep breath. Here I was. The medical staff said he was in intensive care, and we had to be very quick when we went in. I took a deep breath and went in. I had been hopeful he wouldn't make it through the surgery ever since he decided he was going to have the bypass. The gist of this is, the church wouldn't pay for the surgery, but he wanted it, so he signed up for a program through the hospital to get it. Many of you know this program as Medicare. I stood there at his bedside as he put a fake smile on and pretended to be happy to see me. I wanted to scream at that moment, but I had no words for the emotions I was feeling. I stuffed them.

When he survived the bypass surgery, I wondered why a loving God would allow someone like him to continue living but take people capable of kindness and empathy. It didn't make any sense to me.

Even though I had seen Amish doctors, Amish chiropractors, and English chiropractors I was still wetting my bed regularly. I had a chamber pot in my room that I was supposed to use instead of wetting my bed. The problem was the more pressure they put on me to comply with their demands and the more often I was raped in my bed the worse it was. I was afraid to fall asleep. Every time I was hit for not using the chamber pot in my closet instead of wetting my bed, it got worse. The conversations about how I must pray about this and how if I really had faith, I wouldn't be wetting my bed also made it worse. The booklet "To a Girl of Eleven" made me feel so ashamed of existing, I longed to die all the time. I was convinced I would die before I turned thirty.

By some miracle, eventually in this community I was taken to an actual English medical doctor who prescribed me some prescription spray. It helped slightly, but I still wet my bed. I was so ashamed of wetting my bed, I wanted to die. Someone would either kill me or I would find a way to kill myself. I was sinning so hard I was being punished, but what I learned when I finally went to therapy is that it could have been just the symptoms of childhood sexual abuse. It's also interesting that when I escaped, I no longer wet my bed at all. Providing safety and trauma informed care can help with some physical symptoms of childhood trauma as well as trauma therapy from a qualified, licensed trauma therapist.

"Rumspringa"

Rumspringa as defined by the secular world does not exist. We did not call it rumspringa. "We went with the young folks," is what we said.

When I turned seventeen, I was allowed to go to the singings on Sunday night. They were usually at the people's houses that had church that day. Due to us only having church every other Sunday and being such a small community, families would take turns hosting the singing on the in between Sundays. I saw what happened to people when they didn't get baptized when they should, and it was easier to get baptized than experience that in addition to the abuse that was still happening regularly.

I locked my door every night, but it was an old house and there was a small window on top of the door that didn't lock like the rest of the windows. Sometimes I would wake up and someone was in my room. They climbed through the window on top of the door or picked or broke the lock. I always wrapped myself around my blanket and quilt and read books to fall asleep, sometimes someone would be unwrapping me from the blanket and quilt before I realized someone was in my bedroom. There was no safety here.

After the singing is when two boys would take a girl aside to ask her to allow a boy to take them home. If you didn't say yes, you would probably be asked questions about why you said no. If you did say yes, then the boy would hitch his horse to his buggy and drive up the lane to the washhouse and stop, the girl would put on her bonnet or ivakap (winter bonnet) coat, shawl if it was cold and head out to his buggy. It could be a boy she might never have talked to before and off they would go to the girls home, where the girl would be dropped off at the house while the boy would go put up the horse. She would wait for him to come into the house, and they were supposed to sit at the kitchen table , across from each other with an oil lamp lit. For a while they would have a date every two weeks until the boy asked her to go steady. If your family did not approve of the boy, they would encourage you to not continue dating that boy and vice versa for the boy.

It was fast approaching the time when I should get baptized. I observed that people a little older than me did not get baptized when they should have been at 17. I decided that I was going to go "di gma noch" (going after church) after seeing what happened to them. Going di gma noch was supposed to prepare young folks for baptism.

When Sunday came, after the ministry went upstairs and we were singing, the boys going the gma noch first went upstairs in order of age, oldest first. Then the oldest girl got up, and when it was my turn, with my heart pounding in my chest, I felt like throwing up as I dutifully got up and followed upstairs to the room where the ministry was. They had a place for us to sit in a row dutifully as the ministry instructed us in various things.

Going di gma noch went on all summer. One memorable session with the ministry was the one where we promised that if deemed worthy of baptism, we would never tell church business to anyone not a baptized member of the church. At the end of it, the church took a rote (vote) and decided we were worthy of baptism. As I was on my knees in front of the entire congregation with the other candidates for baptism, the Bishop, with a cup and the Deacon, carrying water came around and the Bishop baptized the boys. When it was time for the girls to be baptized, the bishops wife came and carefully removed our kapp and held it while water was poured over our heads, then she placed it carefully back on our head and tied it. One after the other we would answer the three questions that we had to answer to be baptized (one of which was again, a promise not to tell church business to anyone not baptized into the church), and then it was done. I wanted to believe so hard, but by this point I was losing my religion, particularly after reading the Bible several times and being told I couldn't comprehend it, because I was a girl. Remember, women are the weaker vessel, and we are created from a rib.

I was soon going steady with an Amish guy, Henry from another community for over a year. We would go back and forth and write letters. We would always hire van drivers to take us. It was wild though—his community was so liberal. I'd get to play volleyball with the young folks there on Sunday afternoons, before the singings. I loved playing volleyball. There was a certain satisfaction in playing a game like that. I felt the singings they had were better than our own community's and girls had a little more freedom to speak openly in this community. Some of the youth would go roller blading and that was worldly.

Courtship

Courtship rules can vary in many Amish communities. As an example: In my community courtship rules were, when the couple arrived at the girls home, she was to go sit at the kitchen table and the boy was supposed to come to the kitchen and they would sit across from each other for their date until midnight. In Henry's community, the boy was supposed to go in the living room and the girl was supposed to sit on his lap. Old Order Amish community one and two that I lived in practiced bed courtship if I am not mistaken. Old Order Amish community three considered bed courtship to be inviting trouble since the boys and girls going with the young folks would be in bed together one night a week. I don't know what type of courtship Abe Troyer Amish practiced.

One evening after my brother took me to the phone shack to call Henry. On the way home, we stopped at a neighbors place and gathered around the bonfire with English kids our own age. I had a few beers and smoked a few cigarettes. Someone asked me for a picture, and they took pictures of me. I took off my kapp, let my hair down and then they held my dress to my legs as I did a keg stand. There was a crowd of teenagers there drinking underage and I was one of them. After all that, me and my brother snuck home and into our rooms as quietly as we could. We had to get up and chore in the morning, so no one knew we were going to a party. I was so glad when I got up and chored. No one said a word to me about going to a party.

About a month later, one evening after dark there was a knock on the door and Mem got me. She said the armadiena war do fa dich (the deacon was here for you) and I had to talk to them. I stepped outside on the porch with my heart pounding.

Steve the armadiena said "Mary, es var wat gebrockt zu mich es du bischt an en party ganga an da Dick Schafer's haus (Mary, word was brough to me that you went to a party at Dick Schafers house.)

Me: Nae, ich bin net. (No, I did not.)

Steve: Du bischt an en party ganga in Chaseburg. (You went to a party in Chaseburg.)

Me: Nae, ich bin net. (No, I did not.)

Steve: Du bischt an en party ganga. (You went to a party.)

Me: Ya, ich bin. (Yes, I did.)

Steve: Du host hozza aw gedu, smokt, zoffa and di kapp apgnumma. (You wore pants, smoked cigarettes, drank and took off your covering.)

Me: Ich hab smokt, zoffa und di kapp abgnomma, I hab net hozza aw gedu. Ich hab beer ghad, no hab ichts ausglert. Es is net gut. (I did smoke, drink and take off my kapp, I did not put on pants. I had beer and I poured it out. It's not good.)

The conversation continued and I expressed repentance and Steve and his brother Levi said they would take it to the bishop and then be back to tell me wann ich mi sacha recht macha kanna vor di gma (when I can make my things right before the church) after they talk to the bishop.

They came back before our next church Sunday after dark again and informed me that the ministry and Bishop agreed I was repentant and that they would put it to the church on Sunday.

Sunday morning dawned with my stomach falling at the public shaming I knew was coming. The opening song seemed to drag on, the sermon put me to sleep, even gum and candy didn't keep me awake. But finally, the last echoes of the ending song had ended. The bishop had made the announcement where church was to be in two weeks, Lord willing, and instructed all unbaptized to geb di gma platz (give the church space). I went outside with them after they had left and he read off my sins and asked the church to give a rote (vote, but a sham in my opinion since I was told I could only rote with whatever my stepfather and my future husband roted). I stood there by the wash house waiting with my arms crossed, just wishing it all to be over, I had watched people confess before and thought I knew what was coming.

When Steve came and got me to come back, the Bishop informed everyone the church had received further word that I was ungehorsam (disobedient) and several other things and if I agreed to add those to my list of things to repent for I could now get on my knees in front of the men, boys and girls on one side, the bishop in front of me, the woman on the other side. I got on my knees and folded my hands in my lap as I bowed my head. The bishop instructed me to repeat after him:

Ich kann bekenna es ich failed hab, vor Gott und di Gma, verspreche besser sorg traua es noch schae hat bis do her.

I acknowledge that I sinned before God and the church, I promise to better from now on.

The bishop extended his hand to me and welcomed me back to the church. Well, some girls going with the young folks sure did talk about this and they didn't talk to me anymore. At the singings sometimes, girls would whisper together, it was rare anyone would say anything to me except my step-nieces whenever I saw them, they were much nicer to me than the girls in my community.

My stepfather named me this disobedient girl, my Bishop named me as unforgiving, and my mem named me as "just like the English people." That's what the issue was. Even the outsiders that suspected abuse did nothing because it was more important to preserve their business relationship with the Amish community. It seemed hopeless, either I was the cause of my own abuse, torture and terror or I wasn't human enough to be worthy of any intervention from the people that lived with me and around me. Today, I still wonder what kind of human being thinks it is acceptable to place a business relationship above a human life. I also wonder what kind of people would blame their children for being the victims of sexual assault.

While I'm at it here's another thing to consider: I've never pretended to have been a good conforming Amish girl, but at the time I was around maybe eighteen, I snuck away to the neighbors to use their phone. They were watching this documentary on Loretta Lynn, and I heard the stuff that Loretta Lynn went through it really made a significant impact on me to see somebody who went through so many struggles, survived, and thrived.

I used the sheifli (spatula) to scrape the potatoes and make sure they didn't burn as I was frying them over the hot wood stove in the cast iron frying pan. Sweat dripped down my face. It was hot, and we had no air conditioning. I longed to use the kerosene stove instead but obeyed. I heard the door slam loudly and screaming from my stepfather again. My brother rushed past me, then came my stepfather looking mighty baes (angry). I watched as he made a fist and went towards my brother, and I just couldn't anymore. I stood in front of my brother and told him that if he touched me, I was going to report him to the ministry and the law for hitting a church member. He got even angrier, so angry in fact that he jumped up and down in front of me. This time, he didn't hit either of us. He walked away. I am not sure when exactly this happened, but he was sent by the ministry and family to a Plain facility in another state for treatment for his anger and came back with meds, he was supposed to take, which he promptly refused to take once he got back home. It wasn't long before things went back to these episodes of violence being normal occurrences again.

Another episode of violence that struck me as abnormal was watching him hit people and rip their clothing off them, then having a knock on the door and he would answer the door with a smile on his face as if nothing had just happened. This was especially true when it was English people. I was informed not to correct English people. When a driver mentioned some things about rumspringa and I wanted to correct the driver, my mem gave me the "look" I knew meant shut up. So, I was silent and when I got home, Mem said we just let the English think what they will. We don't want them taking our Amish children, so we don't tell them things. It's more important that God knows we are doing the right things.

Sometime later, my brother was taken to that same facility since Mem said we are afraid he's going to run away. I was careful to try to do the right things so I wouldn't get sent there too. To this day, I have night terrors about being taken by Amish people. Specific names that I will not give you, but I think its possible it could be because I watched this happen.

In the summer of 2004, I was riding with my brother and an English driver. There was something said in the vehicle, and I started saying something, my brother just gave me the look, so I was silent. The driver, however, took me aside (I'd known him for about seven years by then) and asked me about what I said.

First, I asked him if this would stay with him. He asked what I meant? I said nobody can know, not the ministry, not the community and most certainly not my family, because I will get in trouble for telling. He promised he would not tell anyone. I don't remember exactly what I said, but enough for him to know I was watching my stepfather hitting us children, including tearing clothing off some of us as well as hitting us with whatever object was around him. He asked me if he could talk to his girlfriend, and they could contact a place where they help people like me. It was terrifying, but I said they could. At the end of a short conversation, I felt more empathy and hope, foreign as they were to me at this point in my life, than I had ever felt before.

A while later, he told me privately that they wondered if he gave me rides, would it be ok to make me an appointment to talk to someone at the center where they help people in situations like this? Again, with a pit in my stomach I shakily said yes. This couple set me up with a Crisis Intervention Center. I ended up going to therapy regularly for the rest of the time I was in this community. The therapist diagnosed me with PTSD eventually. I was nineteen, I felt devastated. My stomach sunk into a bottomless pit of despair as the therapist explained what PTSD was.

When I worked with the people at the center, I met with a counselor. At one point, I mentioned something about telling someone how the crisis intervention center had supported me. The counselor did not want me to share this as they gave me the impression they did not have the resources to support an influx of Amish survivors. At the time I wondered what it was about me that made me worthy of services and not other Amish survivors. However, I have come to understand they knew about the problem in my community and chose to hide from it. But when I showed up courtesy of my English driver, they had no choice but to provide services.

Regardless, I still sometimes wonder what made me worthy of intervention and services over other Amish survivors. The woman in the shop who made a connection with me. The neighbor's child that I played with. My momi who showed me by example that woman can and should stand up for themselves and their families. The one friend whom I shared a love of reading with. The English driver who cared enough to ask what kind of support I needed. The person I met outside of the community from a Plain Mennonite background that was a rock, a role model and believed in me as I navigated my life. All these people made an impact on me that has undeniably shaped my life and I am grateful for their presence in my life.

My Scrapbook with the Forbidden Picture 1

    My stepfather would beat us with anything that was present. I hated it. I saw him hitting people and children around me. It felt scary and hopeless. One day when I got up, my brother didn't come to do chores. When we went to look, he was gone. He had escaped, I missed him every day and had zeitlang (was lonesome) for him. After about a month he came out to visit us and we took a forbidden picture together. It is the only picture I have of me dressed Amish. I missed him, but I was glad he escaped, and it gave me hope that it didn't always have to be like this. When I acquired the printed picture, I carefully put it in my scrapbook, at the very front with a sticker that said "HELP," "Believe in yourself" and "Dreams can happen!"

I'll never forget the day my stepfather walked in the barn and hit our 16-hand high shire gelding with a shovel and our shire gelding turned around and kicked him. Sometimes karma is a 16-hand shire gelding that has had enough.

Sawmill I piled lumber on a few times 1

My muscles were sore from piling lumber on the sawmill, I was glad I wasn't doing it all the time, but someone was sick, so I was helping for a short time. During the summer, I sometimes got to go drive the horses to make hay and help that way. It was a change of pace from the housework and weeding the garden. The horses were great.

I couldn't wait to be done. I had already cleaned the upstairs, washed windows, baked cookies, got told how much time I wasted because even though I was supposed to bake cookies, I did it wrong because I made them with the cookie press instead of dropping cookies with a spoon. My mem was not happy. I wondered to myself, why did we even have a cookie press, but I knew better than saying it aloud.

One of my abusers came to the house and told mem I had to go take his place stacking lumbar on the sawmill, since he didn't feel good. Sure, it's my job to do all my work and get it done quickly in the hope I can go write in my journal or read a book, instead I am now doing the work my abuser gets paid to do and my parents take any money I earn from doing this.

Keeping an eye on the younger children as you went about your assigned tasks was expected of you. Especially, if your parents went somewhere, they would leave older children in charge of the younger children. Sometimes, someone would do something they weren't supposed to (I can't even remember what we did this time) and no one would confess to doing the outlawed deed. Us children would line up in a row, youngest to oldest, and one of our parents would use a rubber hose to hit the youngest child first, because it hurts them to hit us with a piece of a rubber hose and they would hit us until we cried for sure. Sometimes we made it a competition to see who could get hit the most before we cried, 125 hits with that rubber hose were taken by one of us. It was awful to watch our younger siblings cry because they were being hit.

When I was put in charge of my sister Laura, I didn't do the right thing because I didn't spank her. I got into trouble for that, so later I hit her with my hand, pinched/pulled her ears and made her stand in the corner until she stood there for her time. In addition, I would be put in charge of watching out for some of my step nieces and step nephews that were little. If they didn't obey, I was also instructed to hit and I did pinch their ears. I know better now. That was what I was supposed to do to show the children I love them. It is really messed up to realize that love equals inflicting pain on children. I wish I had known better. I know and do better now.

One of the big impacts on me was when my mem asked me if I was planning to marry Henry and I said we had talked about it. My mem told me when I get married, I must do whatever my husband says, whenever he says, inside the bedroom and out. I didn't feel that was right and despaired of ever escaping my fate, continuous pregnancy, an object to be owned and controlled with the voice I would be given by my future husband. I desperately needed a way to escape this fate.

This was further complicated by the pressure from ministry and family to stop seeing my English therapist and go to the Deacon to talk, or even just to an Amish person to empty out. I didn't trust any of the Amish community by this time. I wasn't from a good family or ministry or affluent. Where did I belong, I asked myself?

I also felt upset and angry at the fact that finally for the first time in my life, I could talk in a safe environment and process the terrible events I experienced in a safe way and the people that cared about me wanted me to stop working on PTSD? The dichotomy was not lost to me, it made me more determined to escape my fate.

When my little sister told me word for word what I was told by mem, 13 years earlier, I knew something had to change. I ended up talking to my friend Ashley, who happened to be an Ex-Mennonite, about it. Ashley looked at me and said: Well, what can you live with?

February 16, 2004

Scene: riding as a passenger with one of my abusers and a different English van driver present.

I smell your breath as you lean in and whisper "I have something for you after this car ride"

The overwhelming stench overpowered my senses as I struggled not to wretch.

I think about the other day when you said, "What if we were not brother and sister?"

What do you mean? My stomach churns. My heart pounds. My breath is fast and quick. Will I survive this?

I focused on the radio as we rode in the car. I am alive. I scratch my skin. Yes, I can feel something. I try so hard. I realize, if I don't take this opportunity to run, I will never be safe. I will never be able to keep my sister safe. The rest of the ride home these things run on repeat through my head. I take my things out of the van, mostly. I say hello to my mem and sister. I run upstairs and leave a note. I grab my bag and run outside. I hop in the van with the driver, and we take off, blanketed by darkness on a two-lane road through the countryside in the winter in Wisconsin.

We stop to put a letter detailing abuse in one of our church ministry's mailboxes and I leave my Kapp on the road there. I hop back in, and we take off.

Even today as I write about this: My heart pounds, my eyes well up with tears. How narrowly did I escape? Did the actions I took help my sister?

Escaping was not my last interaction with my family or the church. Leaving was a sin since I was taking the privilege of being born Amish and treading on it. Eventually, I was put in the bann (ban) and meidung (shunned) is practiced. Repercussions were bound to happen, but for the first time in my life I saw some repercussions for those who deserved them instead of the innocent children before me. For some of that story check out Sins of the Amish on Peacock TV.

Shortly after I escaped. I picked up the phone, called the sheriff's department and reported the abuse I experienced. My mem, my stepfather and three of my brothers were arrested. The information from the interview was sent to Pennsylvania. Charges were never brought against my abusers in Pennsylvania.

My notebook has an entry dated April 1, 2004:

"I am so tired and I have a bad headache. The way these Amish punish people is so pathetic. I really wish I could cry again.

My friend's dad thinks its ridiculous.

And this ludicrous rumor I heard about myself only proves how scared these Amish are. "

Star Tribune, April 10, 2004, By Paul Levy 1

Star Tribune, April 10, 2004, By Paul Levy 2

Old Order Amish Four 1998-2004

Amish men waive hearing

By TIM HUNDT
Lee Newspapers

VIROQUA, Wis. — Three Vernon County men facing multiple counts of sexual assault waived their rights Tuesday to a preliminary hearing.
Vernon County District

Gaskell said there could be more charges filed in the case against another person but did not elaborate.
Gaskell said there were two other women who came forward after the charges were filed and claimed they also had been assaulted.

Lacrosse Tribune, April 14, 2004, By Tim Hundt 1

LA CROSSE TRIBUNE
Hometown

Friday, May 14, 2004 — Local and regional news

Men plead with silence
Innocent plea entered on behalf of Amish men charged with sexual assault

By TIM HUNDT
Lee Newspapers

County Circuit Court Wednesday, so the pleas were entered for them by the court. of substantial battery.
Johnny Byler, 25, is charged with five counts of sexual

June 14.
According to court records a fourth man has also been

Lacrosse Tribune, May 14, 2004, By Tim Hundt 1

Brothers accused of trying to flee

By ED HOSKIN
La Crosse Tribune

VIROQUA, Wis. — Two brothers facing sexual assault charges in Vernon County were jailed Monday after being arrested in La Crosse County this past weekend in what authorities said was an attempt to leave Wisconsin.
Eli Byler, 24, and David Byler,

"They were detained on the basis of their statement on where they were headed. There probably will be more charges."

JIM HANSON, Vernon County Undersheriff

Lacrosse Tribune, June 29, 2004, By Ed Hoskins 1

Old Order Amish Four 1998-2004

METRO/STATE
Amish brothers who fled are arrested

Star Tribune, June 29, 2004, By Paul Levy 1

VIROQUA
Man pleads guilty to sexual assault

One of four family members accused of sexually assaulting a woman from their Amish community for years has pleaded guilty to two charges against him.

Wisconsin State Journal, July 2, 2004, Unnamed Reporter 1

Kempf, 78, pleads to lesser charges

Victim speaks: 'You are forever trying to cause trouble with our people'

By MATT JOHNSON
Lee Newspapers

VIROQUA, Wis. — The young woman's words were barely audible in the courtroom filled with Amish people.
Reading from a written statement, she told 78-year-old William Kempf he was

"You are very abusive physically, mentally, verbally and emotionally. You never take any responsibility for your own actions. You are incapable (of) taking advice from anybody. You are mentally unstable."

VICTIM STATEMENT

Lacrosse Tribune, July 8, 2004, By Matt Johnson 1

LA CROSSE TRIBUNE
Hometown B
Monday, July 19, 2004 — Local and regional news — City desk: (608) 791-8218

More Amish women speak out
Vernon County case helps abuse come to light

Old Order Amish Four 1998-2004
Lacrosse Tribune, July 19, 2004, No Reporter listed 1

> "How could this have happened, and is this simply a case of one incredibly dysfunctional family?"
>
> DONALD KRAYBILL, Pennsylvania sociologist

AMISH ABUSE COMES TO LIGHT

From B-1

and child beatings are often ignored or dealt with quietly by elders. In the Wisconsin case, a six-week banishment from the church was deemed sufficient punishment for the repeated assaults.

It's unclear how widespread the abuse is, partly because problems in Amish communities — even those involving

Across green stretches of farmland in Minnesota and Wisconsin, stories of abuse of Amish children have circulated for more than 20 years.

was a common fact," said Mast, who now lives in Almond, Wis. "You didn't talk about it."

Donald Kraybill, a Pennsylvania sociologist who has studied the Amish for 20 years, said the overwhelming majority of the Amish "have happy, positive family relationships."

He noted that between 85 percent and 90 percent of

Lacrosse Tribune, July 19, 2004, No Reporter Listed 2

4B St. Cloud Times   State   Monday, July 19, 2004

Amish women share stories of rape, abuse

Wisconsin case prompts others to come forward

St Cloud Times, July 19, 2004, No Reporter Listed 1

Byler pleads guilty to felony sexual assault

By TIM HUNDT
Lee Newspapers

Lacrosse Tribune, August 5, 2004, By Tim Hundt 1

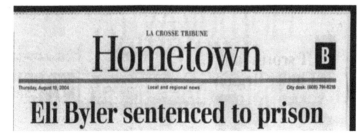

Lacrosse Tribune, August 19, 2004, No Reporter Listed 1

LA CROSSE TRIBUNE
Hometown

Wednesday, September 1, 2004 — Local and regional news — City desk: (608) 791-8218

Byler pleads to sexual assault

Lacrosse Tribune, September 1, 2004, By Tim Hundt 1

Wednesday, October 20, 2004

Byler brother gets 1 year

Lacrosse Tribune, October 20, 2004, By Tim Hundt 1

www.lacrossetribune.com

BYLER SENTENCED

From A-1

Johnny Byler will serve one year in county jail and 10 years probation after pleading guilty to two counts of second-degree sexual assault of a child.

He will be allowed to leave the jail to work and receive counseling and has been ordered to pay $16,700 in restitution and register as a sex offender.

A shaken and sometimes crying Johnny Byler apologized in court: "I hurt a lot of people in this situation. I am sorry to the Amish community. I have given the Amish a very bad name. I am sorry to my wife. I am sorry to

"I hurt a lot of people in this situation. I am sorry to the Amish community. ... I am sorry to my wife. ... I do not want to have any anger in my heart towards anyone because of this situation. I know I have done it to myself."

JOHNNY BYLER, at his sentencing

Lacrosse Tribune, October 20, 2004, By Tim Hundt 2

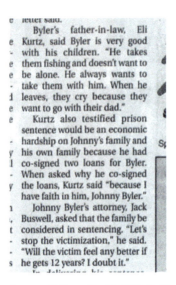

letter said.

Byler's father-in-law, Eli Kurtz, said Byler is very good with his children. "He takes them fishing and doesn't want to be alone. He always wants to take them with him. When he leaves, they cry because they want to go with their dad."

Kurtz also testified prison sentence would be an economic hardship on Johnny's family and his own family because he had co-signed two loans for Byler. When asked why he co-signed the loans, Kurtz said "because I have faith in him, Johnny Byler."

Johnny Byler's attorney, Jack Buswell, asked that the family be considered in sentencing. "Let's stop the victimization," he said. "Will the victim feel any better if he gets 12 years? I doubt it."

Lacrosse Tribune, Oct 20, 2004, By Tim Hundt 3

Byler to join brother in prison for sexual assault

Lacrosse Tribune, November 16, 2004, By Tim Hundt 1

Sexual Abuse in the Amish Community

By ABC News

Aug. 29, 2006 -- "20/20" first aired this story on December 10, 2004

The Amish community is a mysterious world within modern America, a place frozen in another time. The Amish live without automobiles or electricity. Education ends at the eighth grade and life largely centers on farming, family and faith.

Some 90 percent of children raised Amish choose to stay in the community. But one who did not is 22-year-old Mary Byler.

20/20 with Elizabeth Vargas December 10, 2004

Old Order Amish Four 1998-2004

legal affairs — THE MAGAZINE AT THE INTERSECTION OF LAW AND LIFE

► SEARCH   ► DEBATE CLUB   ► ARCHIVES   ► ABOUT US

Features

JANUARY|FEBRUARY 2005

The Gentle People By Nadya Labi
The Last Lord Chancellor? By William Goodhart
Man and the Machines By Benjamin Soskis
Suspect Memories By Jascha Hoffman
Common Denominator By Nicholas Thompson
Money Talks By Andrew Goldstein

THE GENTLE PEOPLE

Impressed by their piety, courts have permitted the Amish to live outside the law. But in some places, the group's ethic of forgive and forget has produced a plague of incest—and let many perpetrators go unpunished.

By Nadya Labi

Legal Affairs Magazine, January/February 2005, By Nadya Labi

Maybe someday, I will find the energy to write about culture shock, court, and the next twenty years of my life.

How can you help?

- Report Abuse to the Law
    - [Every State has a hotline](#) click to find yours
    - It can be reported anonymously

- Educate yourself on current best practice information for prevention of abuse
- Become trauma aware & informed
- Educate yourself on Amish and Anabaptist culture as told by people who lived it (& share this information with professionals and community stakeholders)
- Assist in helping community leaders to have action plans in place prior to crimes being reported
- Print [resources](#) and display or hand them out in public areas such as sale barns, auctions, libraries, court hearings for Amish and Anabaptists etc
- Wear t-shirts that display an educational message
- Every Court Hearing for Amish and Anabaptist folks is an educational opportunity
- [Sign this petition](#) to help give abused children in America access to language and resources to be able to report abuse as well as receive trauma informed support
- Provide financial support for organizations combatting child abuse

Epilogue

Today I still smoke cigarettes and I've worn a few pairs of pants. I still enjoy the fresh baked smell and taste of yeast bread and make it for myself.

Beer is still not something I consume as its disgusting. I do, however, occasionally enjoy a glass of wine.

I love to paint, sew, draw, and write.

Nature is a wonderful place to explore, and I often find solace in nature. It is a great place for me to feel at one with my surroundings.

My music tastes have strayed a bit from just the Loretta Lynn, Conway Twitty and Old Country I listened to under the covers. Currently, my latest favorite bands are Citizen Soldier, Sky Dxddy and Halsey. Somedays, I might even be listening to Mozart or Alternative and Heavy Metal. I'm in love with music and stim regularly with music in my home and while working.

I invite you to check out some of my Poetry, Paintings and Sewing in the following pages.

Writings and Art

"Art is to console those who are broken by life."

— *Vincent Van Gogh*

Starting Over

By: Mary Byler

I cry.

I scream.

I cry.

You will not break me.

You will not manipulate me.

I'm going to start my real life.

Away from the stifling area where there is no way to breathe.

Starting my life.

A life where love exists.

A life where I'm free.

A life where no one gets to control me.

A life where I get to choose connections and bonds that mean something to me.

Filled with joy, love, and light.

A life where compassion, kindness and humor exist.

A life where I am a human being, with human rights.

A life where I have human rights.

A life where I am celebrated for existing.

A life where I am valued, my feelings are honored, and I am safe.

Lie For You

Mary Byler, 2004

I scream, I'm terrified

My brothers lied

My mom, believed them

Over me.

Now I'll have to see, the heart wrenching price I'll pay

All because I'll never say: "I lied"

You lied, what you did is horrible

My innocence you stole

My innocence is gone

Cause what you did was wrong

My trust, you destroyed

As you raped me on my bed

My hopes you dashed to the ground

When you lied, I was bound.

Because you're controlled by your lust (for power and control)

My eyes, you've filled with tears

You drank so many beers

And my body pays the price

You're more horrifying than lice

My life you've made into a hell

Your soul you would sell

For a little lust, a little control over a child, that you can rule, that you can overcome with power, you make my mouth turn sour, with distaste for your treatment of me. Now I believe, now I see, you are so weak, you cannot speak, you must force your lust on a child, and you are ugly, mean, dirty and vile.

Little Girl

22 January 2006

By Mary Byler

I can't breathe, let me go, let me go…

I screamed…

I can't see, let me go, let me go…

…but nobody heard, nobody cared,

They went right on holding my dress…

…above my head…And holding it shut…

…With my arms inside the dress with me…

…So, I can't see…I can't fight…I can't breathe…

…I'm suffocating…and nobody cared…nobody…mommas' boys, (she can't hear although I'm screaming as loud as I can) daddy's dead… (Thank God what daddy did was worse) ...

…let me go, I scream as I'm gasping for air…

…please let me go, I'll never get in your way…

"God, if you make them let me go, I'll be so good, I'll never do anything bad again…I'll never get mad, Please God make them let me go…God didn't care either."

…Nobody cares about me, I'm all alone in the world and they touch…me where they shouldn't…they do bad things to me all the time and

…no one cares…

…No one understands…

…No one loves me…

…No one wants me…

…all alone. Crying myself to sleep…every night…

…wishing God would let me die…

…cause nobody cares…

> I'm so ashamed of my body…
>
> Surely no one else ever has this happen…
>
> Mommy says, "You can never ever tell anyone."

Mommy also said

> "You don't pray hard enough"
>
> And
>
> "You don't fight hard enough."

Mommy said that

> "If you truly never want anything like this to happen it won't."
>
> And that
>
> "God must be punishing you."

I don't understand why does God let this happen to me…when I try so hard to be good..

I'm all alone…a scared little girl…

Trying to be brave and live through this…

–huddling and shivering under the covers as I cry myself to sleep…

…one more day, that I'm all alone and no one cares what happens…

So, there I am all alone and terrified of the world…

A tiny little girl…

Who am I?

By: Mary Byler, 2021

I am Mary.

I am a child.

I am unsafe.

I am alone.

I have no one.

I am blamed.

I am ashamed.

I am dismissed.

I am nothing.

I am going to grow up and marry a woman.

I am screaming in the abyss. HELP!

I am crying as my heart breaks from the hurt from my egg donor.

No one helps.

I am the daughter who was never quite enough, or right enough.

I am the sister, never more than an object to be used for men's gratification.

I am the aunt, not quite the same as others, too blunt and direct to be acceptable.

I am speaking the words until people do their job instead of dismissing me because Amish people will never commit such crimes.

I am NOT SILENT.

I AM NOT CONFORMING.

I am a parent.

I am my heart breaking as I realize, "I was a child."

I deserved to be safe.

I deserved to be loved

I deserved to be accepted for who I am.

I deserved to have proper nutrition

I still do.

I deserve the same consideration and compassion I give to others.

I deserve to be treated with openness and honesty.

I deserve integrity and conversation.

I am not to be mistaken for a compliant (or presenting compliant) AMISH girl.

I am so much more than my egg donor led me to believe.

I am human.

I am worthy.

I am no better and no worse than anyone else.

I am enough.

I am a parent.

I am a lover.

I am a warrior.

I am me!

I am free!

NO, F*** YOU

Mary Byler 2022

I was worthy,

I was enough,

I was truthful,

I was loving,

I was kind,

I was modest,

I was faithful,

I was a believer,

I was compassionate,

I was grateful,

I was generous,

I was forgiving,

I was abused,

I was silent when the abuse escalated,

I was told, "if you truly didn't want stuff to happen to you, it wouldn't keep happening to you."

I was told "if you truly had faith, believed enough and prayed enough, this stuff wouldn't keep happening to you."

I was unsafe.

I was a child.

I was alone, yet surrounded by PEOPLE, some of whom suspected or knew of the abuse, no one provided meaningful intervention that led to safety.

If you're around people that you suspect are abusing children, what action do you take?

Coming Out
Mary Byler 2022

Did you see how much I tried to be with you?

I cared about you, but she beckoned me with her eyes

Her smile

Her words

Her body

Her spirit

Her soul

I kneel before you as I pushed the thoughts of her aside.

I begged for your love to be like hers.

Desperate.

I didn't know.

You couldn't be what I needed.

I couldn't be what you deserved.

And I cried.

And I begged you to be your friend.

Still

She beckoned me with her kindness and her softness.

Her hand in mine, held on tight.

She walked beside me every night.

Every step.

She sees me as I am.

Night terrors.

Flashbacks,

Sleeping problems,

Caring,

Compassionate,

Working to overcome,

Loving,

Passionate,

Always fighting to survive, what was done to me against my will.

She sees me.

She loves me.

And I am ENOUGH.

My drawing of a rose with a lead pencil

Quilt I made

Shirt I made

Some of the things I drew when I felt awful in 2003 and 2004

My Emotions painting, I made in 2021

Thanks for Reading!

Name card I would pass out when I went with the young folks

About the Author

Art by BJK 1

Mary Byler is the Manager and Founder of The Misfit Amish, an organization dedicated to providing secular support and resources to Amish and ex-Amish survivors. As an educator and advocate for Amish children, she collaborates with other organizations and agencies to provide best practice-based resources for Amish/Plain communities and survivors. A medical coder by profession, Byler also holds a Master certificate in life coaching, multiple certifications in trauma awareness, and specializes in working with survivors from cults and conservative sectarian religious groups. She is certified in social and behavioral research by the Collaborative Institutional Training Initiative and is a researcher and cultural advisor for the Lock Haven University study on child sexual abuse in conservative Anabaptist communities. Byler was a co-creator of a recent exhibit in Lancaster County on Amish/Plain clothing and sexual assault. She produces audio and video recordings of Amish/Plain survivor stories, with a focus on LGBTQ survivor stories.

Made in the USA
Coppell, TX
01 May 2023